SPECULATORS

For my Mum and Dad

TONY MARCHANT

SPECULATORS

AMBER LANE PRESS

All rights whatsoever in this play are strictly reserved and
application for performance, etc. should be made before
rehearsal to:
Lemon and Durbridge Ltd.
24 Pottery Lane
Holland Park
London W11 4LZ

No performance may be given unless a licence has been
obtained.

First published in 1988 by
Amber Lane Press Ltd.
9 Middle Way
Oxford OX2 7LH

Typeset in Ehrhardt by Oxford Computer Typesetting

Printed and manufactured in Great Britain by
Cotswold Press Ltd., Eynsham, Oxford

Copyright © Tony Marchant, 1988

ISBN: 0 906399 90 4

CHARACTERS

ALEX SOUTH: *an American banker*
GATEKEEPER: *doorman at the Bank of England*
ROBIN PENBURY: *an official at the Bank of England*

Foreign exchange dealers:
JIMMY
IAN
NICK
SARAH
GRAHAM CUTTER

CHARLIE CROSS: *chief dealer*
JULIE: *a Telex girl*
A BROKER
ANNIE: *a wine-bar-maid*
CAROL CUTTER: *Graham's wife*
MR. MILLAR: *Sarah's father*

Speculators was first presented at The Pit, London, on 9th December, 1987. It was directed by Barry Kyle with the following cast:

ALEX SOUTH:	Philip O'Brien
GATEKEEPER:	Stanley Dawson
ROBIN PENBURY:	Richard Bremmer
JIMMY:	Gary Love
IAN:	Howard Ward
NICK:	Simon Russell Beale
SARAH:	Amanda Harris
GRAHAM CUTTER:	Gerard Murphy
CHARLIE CROSS:	Robert Demeger
JULIE:	Nimmy March
A BROKER:	Roger Moss
ANNIE:	Jane Lancaster
CAROL CUTTER:	Di Botcher
MR. MILLAR:	Raymond Bowers

Designed by Fotini Dimou

Lighting by Wayne Dowdeswell

Music composed by Jeremy Sams

Sound by Alastair Goolden

ACT ONE

SCENE ONE

The reception area of the Bank of England. A GATEKEEPER, *dressed in a black silk topper, salmon pink swallow-tail coat, bright red waistcoat, black tie and white shirt, is searching* ALEX SOUTH, *an American banker, dressed in a grey suit.*

SOUTH: I do have an appointment.

KEEPER: Security, sir . . . it's the same for everyone . . . I hope you don't mind.

SOUTH: You're the Gatekeeper?

KEEPER: Yes, sir.

SOUTH: Where are the guys who normally do this?

KEEPER: Tea break, sir.

[*Pause.*]

SOUTH: You're part of the Bank of England's tradition, right?

KEEPER: Yes, sir — it goes back a long way.

SOUTH: To what?

KEEPER: Beg your pardon, sir?

SOUTH: What is the tradition — that it goes back a long way to?

KEEPER: Well, it . . . I . . . er can't say as I can really help you on that one, sir.

SOUTH: You don't know? You're part of a tradition but you don't know what it is — is that right?

KEEPER: Can you open your briefcase for me, please, sir?

SOUTH: You wouldn't get me dressed up like that without a damn good reason why.

KEEPER: I've got a good reason, sir.

SOUTH: What's that?

KEEPER: It's traditional. It's traditional and that's good enough for me. Attendants such as myself create an impression on visitors, sir, create confidence in the Bank of England as an institution of long standing. Respect too, sir. We're an imposing sight when they enter.

SOUTH: Well, as you can see, I'm struck with awe.

KEEPER: Struck with what, sir?

SOUTH: Nothing. Forget it. [*Pause.*] What if I told you there was a gun hidden in there?

> [*He indicates the briefcase. The* GATEKEEPER *is suddenly wary.*]

KEEPER: What's going on?

SOUTH: Nothing. It's just a hypothetical question.

KEEPER: Oh. [*Pause.*] Well, it would be beholden on me to call the security staff, sir.

SOUTH: What if they weren't here? Like now. What if I pulled it out and started waving it about? Would you try to disarm me?

KEEPER: No sir, I'm not qualified.

SOUTH: What would you do, then?

KEEPER: I'd probably be taking a position behind that pillar, sir.

SOUTH: You'd hide?

KEEPER: In a manner of speaking.

SOUTH: You wouldn't be a very imposing sight, cowering there, would you? Confidence in the Bank would go right out of the window.

KEEPER: I'm not a policeman, sir. I'm symbolical of the Bank. As an institution.

SOUTH: But you'd be disappearing behind that pillar at the first sign of trouble — what kind of symbolism is that? And as for the tradition that you're part of — it's a mystery to you. You know, I'm surprised there's not a run on the pound more often.

KEEPER: Look, mate, it's just a bleeding job!

> [ROBIN PENBURY, *a Bank of England official, arrives.*]

PENBURY: Alex, sorry to have kept you.

SOUTH: It's O.K. . . . I've just been helping your attendant through an identity crisis.

KEEPER: The gentleman was wondering about the origins of the costume, sir . . . and our function.

SOUTH: [*to* PENBURY] Can you help?

PENBURY: Sorry . . . history's not my strong point.

SOUTH: Well, as I understand it they were liveried servants of the first Governor of the Bank of England, Sir John

Houblon, who was a member of the famous Huguenot family. That would mean they were introduced around 1694. However, the dress of the servants cum messengers apparently dates from the early nineteenth century and is thought to have been designed by Sir John Soane, 1788-1833, the architect who also designed the Bank's reception hall — the place that we're standing in right now.

> [*Pause.* PENBURY *and the* GATEKEEPER *look at each other.*]

Nobody knows more about British history than an American. Strange, really, because we're not particularly fond of the past. Especially our own. We're always trying to give it a face-lift.

KEEPER: Your briefcase, sir.

> [*The* GATEKEEPER *hands the briefcase back to* SOUTH *and is about to go.*]

SOUTH: Here.

> [*He tips the* GATEKEEPER.]

An old American tradition — no one does anything for anyone else without they get a dollar bill thrust into their hand first.

> [*The* GATEKEEPER *goes.*]

[*to* PENBURY] Maybe you're just lulling visitors into a false sense of security. Behind the quaint customs a computer room is humming, right?

PENBURY: You're in a very confrontational mood this morning.

SOUTH: I'm ready for this meeting, Robin.

PENBURY: Sit down, Alex. The Directors are still at lunch. We have a few moments. [*Pause.*] The loan you put together for the airline for the 747's . . . quite conditional, wasn't it?

SOUTH: It was an attractive package. A cut price leasing deal. No one else was big enough to come up with a better offer.

PENBURY: There was a rather alarming power of veto in it, however. You demanded a say in their next choice of aircraft manufacturer.

SOUTH: It was called driving a hard bargain.

PENBURY: Some might call it an outrageous interference.

SOUTH: The airline didn't — they took the money.
PENBURY: They weren't in a position to refuse it. [*Pause.*] Now their medium-haul planes need replacing soon. The hope is that they'll buy British.
SOUTH: That depends on what we think.
PENBURY: We understand you're wanting the order to go to Seattle.
SOUTH: Makes sense to us.
PENBURY: The European plane is better.
SOUTH: You sound like the DTI. I hope you're not going to go and get all political on me.
PENBURY: There is a national interest at stake here. Airbus is counting on getting the order — the job losses in the UK could run into thousands otherwise.
SOUTH: Has the airline been crying on your shoulder?
PENBURY: They're worried about the political flak such a decision would attract.
SOUTH: Why should they give a fuck about the national interest — they're privatised now.
PENBURY: Old habits die hard.
SOUTH: The market's king.
PENBURY: But you're choosing for them!
SOUTH: No, we're just prepared to exercise the right of veto.
PENBURY: From the safety of some boardroom in Chicago? I expect the British aircraft industry and its workers are invisible to the naked eye from there.
SOUTH: Let's not get emotive. All considerations are financial ones. Are the DTI getting involved in this?
PENBURY: The takeover bid's at the Monopolies and Mergers Commission. It isn't seemly for them to intervene again.
SOUTH: So it's your turn to put pressure on us?
PENBURY: You and I are supposed to have a relationship, Alex.
SOUTH: What do you want?
PENBURY: Give up your veto. Let the airline decide which plane it leases.
SOUTH: We're not complete shits. We're quite happy for the engines to be British.
PENBURY: But for how long?

SOUTH: Rolls Royce is safe for the time being. Look, I don't see why we should be dog in the manger here. We're handing out the money, we're taking risks.

PENBURY: You're acting like loan sharks.

SOUTH: The days of British industry borrowing from British banks are over. You can't deregulate and have economic sovereignty. I thought the money markets would have taught you that. Sir John and Sir Jack can't arrange anything on the ninth tee any more because Nomura and Goldman Sachs are shouting fore and playing through.

PENBURY: Why are you so keen on the American plane?

SOUTH: All considerations are financial ones.

PENBURY: I know your bank's taken a fourteen per cent shareholding in the manufacturer, Alex.

SOUTH: We underwrite them — why shouldn't we own a piece of them?

PENBURY: You lend money to a British airline on condition that it only buys from a manufacturer that you own? That's not the free market at work, that's bloody despotism.

SOUTH: Surely you're under some illusion — the market's not about competition, it's about control. To get big enough to do whatever the fuck you like.

[*Pause.*]

PENBURY: More than ever, Alex, we have to be seen to be ... regulating. Now when we want to stop McDonalds or whoever from acquiring, say, the Midland Bank, we simply make our objections known. That usually does the trick.

SOUTH: Not here it doesn't.

PENBURY: Yes and in ... difficult cases we sometimes find that matters can only be resolved by the Bank facing up to its ... statutory responsibilities. We have a power of veto too, Alex. One the market doesn't possess.

SOUTH: A power you wouldn't dare exercise.

PENBURY: Against improper practices ... I think so.

SOUTH: You've decided you don't like what you see all of a sudden. The City hasn't got new overnight — it's sixteen years since Bretton Wood ended and the foreign exchange market started. One look at that could have told you the shape of things to come. You should see the kids I've got dealing in it — they're quite at home with liberalisation.

SCENE TWO

The foreign exchange dealing room of a bank. There are six consoles or stations, which can either be arranged in a circular fashion or at right angles to each other like desks. (Often they are joined up, three in a line, but this may present staging difficulties.) Across the way is a separate station, which is known as the 'Corporate Desk'. This is (wo)manned by SARAH. *Each station or console consists of two phones, a bank of buttons and a small screen (perhaps one between two). There are clocks giving the time of day in each of their major world markets: New York, Hong Kong, Singapore, Frankfurt. In London it is 7.15 a.m. The* DEALERS *are at their stations. One of them,* JIMMY, *is up, looking out of the window. He turns to the others.*

JIMMY: Most people are just waking up now. All the joes, wandering about in their pyjamas, putting their bad breath over a bowl of cereal. I mean, here we are with the fate of the world's currencies in our hands and they ain't even bought their train tickets yet. They think business only lasts from nine till going home time. Our market never stops. [*shouts out of the window*] They're still dealing in Asia. It's half-past four in Hong Kong. Tea-time.

[IAN *gets up to see who* JIMMY *is shouting at.*]

IAN: [*to the others*] There's a postman down there looking a bit puzzled.

NICK: Funny you should be espousing the wonders of the global market, seeing as you don't trust anybody north of Rotherhithe.

JIMMY: But it's special, though — what we do.

IAN: What's so special about getting up early? My dad used to have to get up at four o'clock in the morning.

JIMMY: Why – was he an insomniac?

IAN: No, he was on early shift at the steel plant. Till he got made redundant. He's an insomniac now.

JIMMY: Tell him to count sheep. [*Pause.*] What d'you do in bed Sarah . . . when you can't sleep?

SARAH: Think about you . . . you're like Valium with a tie on.

JIMMY: I'm like a broom handle in the mornings.

SARAH: Shut up you little shit.

NICK: I love the level of sophistication in this room, don't you? One minute we're reacting to trade deficit forecasts and the next we're addressing the concept of fuck, shit and piss.

IAN: Trouble with you is you like to make this business sound more high-falutin' than it really is. Jimmy comes on like he's Armand Hammer and you pretend you need a Ph.D. in macro-economics. It's just pass the parcel. [*to* JIMMY] D'you remember when that waiter was rude to him on his holiday in Madrid? He came back all upset and said, "Let's start a run on the peseta."

JIMMY: That's right — "Sell ten quids' worth," he said, "and put a rumour into the brokers that their king's been shot."

NICK: Quite right too — their central bank would have been wetting themselves. [*Pause.*] Swarthy little tyke wouldn't serve me.

SARAH: Is that what's meant by market sentiment?

JIMMY: [*indicating* CUTTER] Look at him over there, look — hasn't said a word since we came in. The man's a prince, he's above all this bickering. He's just concentrating on the screen, watching the way the prices are moving. Ears to the brokers' boxes, listening to what's coming out of there. He's a fox and a leopard. I tell ya, that's me in a few years' time. The cable dealer. Best seat in the room.

CUTTER: What am I — the Cincinnati Kid?

JIMMY: Close.

NICK: At my school once you'd have been his fag.

CUTTER: I'd have stuck you in my ear and saved you for later.

NICK: Typical youth . . . he thinks the cable desk is glamorous.

CUTTER: He's right.

JIMMY: Anyway, wouldn't you like to be on three per cent dealer's commission of his profit?

NICK: I'm not his poor cousin — I deal dollar/mark, remember?

JIMMY: Yeah, but when the crash happened who made most out of it, eh? When all those wankers in the Stock Market were writing out their wills, Graham bought Sterling at one-sixty-eight and watched it go up to one-seventy-two before unloading. You didn't even get into a position on marks.

NICK: Yes I did. I'll punch you in a minute.

IAN: The shit will hit the fan.

JIMMY: Why did all those bastards in braces bottle out?

CUTTER: They weren't used to crises.

JIMMY: We are, though, eh?

CUTTER: The pound has moved seventy cents against the dollar in the last two and a bit years.

NICK: That's what you call a floating exchange system.

IAN: Adrift, more like.

SARAH: The markets know best.

IAN: The most surprising thing about October was that people were surprised by it.

JIMMY: But there'll always be a future for us in FX, won't there?

IAN: The Christmas lights in the Square Mile might dim from time to time but they'll never go out. The rest of the country might look like it's having a nuclear winter . . .

[*The others chime in with a chorus of "Boring".*]

NICK: We don't want any of that crank politics here, thank you very much.

JIMMY: Here, I hear the Labour Party's got a new venue for next year's Conference — it's booked a room above the 'Horse and Groom'.

NICK: 'Democratic Socialism — where now?' — Guest speaker: Hilda Ogden.

SARAH: I went to this new place down by the docks last night; it's called the 'Tolpuddle Brasserie'.
[*A look from* IAN.]
Only joking.
[CHARLIE CROSS, *the Chief Dealer, arrives.*]

CROSS: Morning, team.

JIMMY: All right, coach.

CROSS: Positions, anyone?

JIMMY: Flat.

IAN: Me too.

NICK: I'm ten long on dollars. Bank of Wisconsin sold me some.

CUTTER: There's no trends in the market. Just playing it on people's positions.

CROSS: What was the closing bid for cable in Hong Kong last night?

CUTTER: One-seventy-three-twenty. It hasn't moved much in Hong Kong since.

CROSS: This thing in the Gulf — d'you think it's worth getting into a position on?

CUTTER: Market's getting immune to ships being blown up.

JIMMY: If this Iran-Iraq war carries on, is it bad for the dollar, then?

CUTTER: It'd be bad for Sterling if it ever ended.

JIMMY: How's that?

CUTTER: There'd be more oil production.

NICK: Cheaper prices.

SARAH: Less export revenue for the UK.

JIMMY: Fucking Arabs.

CROSS: We don't take sides, Jimmy — we just make sure that if they threaten peace we're not long on Sterling. If we ever do something that's out of step with the rest of the market, we're fucked.

IAN: We take the moral stance of the arms dealer, i.e. we don't have one. We don't take sides, we just take positions so we can put money in either pocket.

CROSS: [*to* IAN] Your light's on.
[IAN *picks up the phone. He listens, then . . .*]

IAN: Russians looking for a Sterling/mark in twenty quid.

[*The others look on at* NICK *for his response.*]

NICK: [*to* CUTTER] What's the cable at the moment?

CUTTER: Thirty/forty.

NICK: Make it seventy/eighty for twenty quid.

IAN: [*down the phone*] Seventy/eighty. [*coming back to* NICK] Taken at eighty!

NICK: [*American accent*] That's sixty-seven million marks due from the Foreign Trade Bank of Moscow.

CROSS: What d'you think?

CUTTER: Might be a spoof. Buying a little to push the price up, then selling a lot.

CROSS: Maybe they just think Sterling's going to go up.

CUTTER: Fucking communists — they make more money out of this game than anyone.

NICK: It's a party — everyone's invited.

CUTTER: I'll get in touch with Boris direct — see what he's up to.
  [*He taps out on a keyboard and contacts the Foreign Trade Bank of Moscow via his computerised dealing screen. Pause.*]
  I think Boris is buying Sterling/mark elsewhere, Nick.

CROSS: Price isn't moving much.

CUTTER: Soon see. It's going up. The Russians are on a big buying operation, I know it. We'd better jump on their bandwagon.
  [CROSS *hesitates.*]
  What's the matter, Charlie — don't you trust me?

CROSS: You're the cable dealer.

CUTTER: That's right.

NICK: [*approving*] Ship that Sterling in!

CUTTER: Can I have some cable calls, please? Right-hand side.
  [NICK, JIMMY *and* IAN *get on the phones. We hear them almost simultaneously enquiring.*]

NICK: What are you calling cable, please?

IAN: Can I have a spot for cable, please?

JIMMY: Cable quote!
  [CUTTER *waves his hand forward every time a call is made.*]

NICK: Fifty/fifty-five!

CUTTER: Take ten!

NICK: [*down the phone*] Ten mine!

IAN: Fifty-eight/sixty-three!

CUTTER: Take ten. Quickly, the price is going to go up in a minute.

IAN: Mine! Ten quid I buy.

JIMMY: Fifty-eight . . . sixty-eight!

CUTTER: I told you. Tell him to fuck off and die.

JIMMY: Fuck off and·die.

CUTTER: Come on, more calls, please.

NICK: What are you calling cable?

IAN: Can I have a spot for cable!

JIMMY: Level for cable!

NICK: Fifty-seven/sixty-four!

CUTTER: Ten mine.

NICK: Ten at sixty-four!

IAN: Fifty-eight/sixty-three!

CUTTER: Take ten.

IAN: Ten mine.

JIMMY: Sixty-two/seventy-two!

CUTTER: No thank you.

JIMMY: [*down the phone*] No.

NICK: Fifty-eight/sixty-three!

CUTTER: Take ten.

NICK: Ten mine!

JIMMY: Fifty-nine/sixty-four!

CUTTER: That's it.

IAN: Fifty-eight/sixty-seven.

CUTTER: That's enough.

[*They all record the deals on their trading slips.*]

CROSS: What was that — six calls?

CUTTER: I'm fifty quid long, now. Let's see how high it'll go.

JIMMY: We're getting eighty-five Sterling bid now, Graham.

CROSS: Twenty point profit if you take it now. It won't go any higher. Come on.

[CROSS *and* CUTTER *share a look.*]

CUTTER: I don't need prodding, Charlie. I've been doing this a long time. [*to the others*] Let's turn it round, then, let's get out!

[*They all get on the phones again. With every sell,*

CUTTER *jabs his hand forward. The shouts may have to run into each other.*]

NICK: What are you calling cable?

IAN: Cable price, please.

JIMMY: Cable quote.

NICK: Eighty-three/ninety!

CUTTER: Ten yours!

NICK: Ten yours!

IAN: Eighty-seven/ninety-five!

CUTTER: Done at eighty-seven!

IAN: Ten yours!

JIMMY: Ninety/ninety-seven!

CUTTER: Given!

JIMMY: Given at ninety!

NICK: What are you calling cable!

IAN: Cable price, please!

JIMMY: Cable quote!

NICK: Ninety/figure!

CUTTER: Yours!

NICK: Yours!

IAN: Eighty-seven/ninety-two!

[CUTTER *just shows with his hand this time.*]
Given!

JIMMY: Ninety-five/figure!

CUTTER: Yours and I'm out!

JIMMY: Yours and he's out! [*down the phone*] Sorry.

[*They all fill out their trading slips.* CROSS *checks the details on each of them.*]

NICK: Nice little bubble, wasn't it?

IAN: You and the Russians have pushed the pound up half a cent now.

NICK: What d'you make there?

CUTTER: About seventy grand.

NICK: Seventy grand in three minutes. No wonder banks like us have got the tallest buildings in London.

JIMMY: Poetry in motion, ain't he?

IAN: [*caustic*] Fuck poetry — we're talking wealth creation.

CUTTER: A thirty point profit, Charlie, not twenty.

CROSS: Good move.

[CROSS *goes into his office.*]

NICK: The comrades did you a favour.

JIMMY: You're just jealous 'cause he beat the market. I wouldn't have seen that bubble starting.

SARAH: That's why he's the cable dealer and you're on Australian dollar.

JIMMY: Will you suck my cock when I'm sitting there, Sarah?

SARAH: I love the way he plays but he's not juicy.

CUTTER: Thanks very much.

SARAH: Anyway, Jimmy, it'll be years before you're sitting there.

JIMMY: I'm learning all the time.

CUTTER: It's just poker with knobs on.

IAN: That's right.

NICK: What knobs?

CUTTER: A Reuter's screen, a broker's box, two telephones and the international banking community. . .

NICK: I thought we were going to hear a cosy working-class homily about how it's all a bit like working 'dahn the stools on Levver Lane'.

JIMMY: If you hate the working class so much how come you live in Wapping?

NICK: In Chelsea everyone else was rich. Living in the midst of the poor you feel like an absolute millionaire.

CUTTER: Anyway, listening to you anyone would think I was the Terry Venables of British finance.

JIMMY: A day don't go by without another bank offering him a job. All over the City they want him as their cable dealer.

NICK: I get taken to lunch too, y'know.

IAN: My Porsche is newer than your Porsche.

[JULIE, *the Telex girl, enters. She starts to pick up the trading slips from the* DEALERS' *trays.*]

NICK: Julie, my darling, if you were a currency I'd have twenty quids' worth.

JIMMY: Yours! Done at two bob.

JULIE: Fuck off —

SARAH: [*on the phone, calling over*] Ten dollars dollar/mark for Courtaulds.

[JULIE *drops a trading slip on the floor. In a tight*

> *skirt, she reaches down to retrieve it, her buttocks prominent.*]

JIMMY: Looks like there's a full moon out tonight —

NICK: Well, being a romantic I'd like to be under it.

SARAH: Ten dollars dollar/mark in competition!

> [NICK *is now whispering something in* JULIE's *ear. She doesn't seem overly impressed.*]

I want a price, wanker! Arrange to fuck her later.

> [NICK *is barracked by the other* DEALERS. JULIE *looks angrily at* SARAH.]

NICK: [*a little sheepish*] Twenty/thirty!

SARAH: [*down the phone*] Twenty/thirty! No good. They've dealt elsewhere.

NICK: Sorry.

SARAH: Sorry isn't going to give us turnover. One of our biggest corporate customers is yelling down the phone and I'm having to wait for your hard-on to go down.

JIMMY: [*to* IAN] Wouldn't fancy meeting her on a dark night, would you?

NICK: [*to* SARAH] Funny you should be so interested in my penis — you're growing one yourself, aren't you? How's it coming along?

JIMMY: Nick, Deutsche Bank, Stuttgart . . . five bucks . . .

NICK: Twenty/twenty-five!

JIMMY: Twenty/twenty-five! [*Pause.*] Lose five! Any idea what time these unemployment figures are out?

IAN: Why — you can't get into a position on them.

CUTTER: If they're up, the market wouldn't take any notice anyway. If they was down, everyone'd know the figures had been fiddled. 'S'why I always go in flat.

IAN: Why's he interested, then?

JIMMY: It's my social concern.

NICK: He's got a bet with me. I reckon they'll be up fifteen thousand, he reckons twenty. Twenty-five quid to the winner.

IAN: Words fucking fail me. They do really.

> [JULIE *approaches* SARAH.]

JULIE: Please don't embarrass me like that again, Sarah. It's bad enough having to put up with them, without you joining in.

SARAH: That was a ten million dollar trade we should have been in then. I was more interested in that than sparing your blushes. Anyway, you're a Telex girl — you should be used to it by now.

JULIE: I thought you'd understand. My mistake.

[*Pause.*]

SARAH: Look, I'm sorry about . . .

JULIE: Forget it.

[*She exits. The others have witnessed this.*]

JIMMY: That's right, Sarah, you tell her. Whingeing women, eh? Pain in the arse.

CUTTER: Sarah, d'you think that Scottish Widows call was part of a larger order?

SARAH: Yes I do.

CUTTER: The dollar's started rising. I think they've put it through Barclays, who must be getting into a position on it.

JIMMY: How d'you know?

CUTTER: I've just been listening to their favourite broker. Calls, everyone!

JIMMY: He's the best in London, he's fucking blinding!

NICK: [*down the phone*] What are you calling cable!

IAN: [*down the phone*] Cable price, please!

JIMMY: [*down the phone*] Cable level!

SCENE THREE

Wine bar. Lights up as JIMMY *is arranging one champagne glass on top of another. He is watched by* IAN *and* NICK. SARAH *turns from the bar to join them. They are in high spirits.* CUTTER *is at the bar talking to the young woman,* ANNIE, *who works there. Two empty bottles of champagne stand on a table next to* JIMMY.

IAN: [*to* JIMMY] You're like a kid with a new toy.

SARAH: What's this — his party piece?

NICK: I remember when his sort were happy with a brown ale
and a game of darts.

JIMMY: Well, that's progress, innit?

SARAH: Nick's pissed off because the upper classes don't have
the monopoly on vulgarity any more.

NICK: Quite right — now any self made yob can wreck a posh
restaurant. It's taken all the fun out of it.

IAN: That's the freedom of opportunity we're all so lucky to
enjoy now. Joys of democracy, eh? We do this sort of
thing all the time in Rotherham y'know. The local
shops are running out of champagne glasses there.

JIMMY: Shut up everybody, you're putting me off. This is a
really good trick when it gets going.

> [*Having made the pyramid, he starts to pour cham-
> pagne into the top glass. It overflows into the glass
> below and so on till the pouring achieves a kind of
> waterfall effect. A* BROKER *appears, holding a bottle
> of champagne.*]

NICK: Man with a mission.

SARAH: [*alerting*] Graham . . .

JIMMY: What's he after?

NICK: Hope.

CUTTER: [*greeting the* BROKER] How's tricks?

BROKER: [*to* ANNIE] Another glass please, young lady.

CUTTER: Annie, this is . . .

ANNIE: [*interrupting*] Yes, we've met.

BROKER: Hello . . . again. [*Pause. to* CUTTER] You know why I've
come.

CUTTER: To make me an offer I can't refuse?

ANNIE: [*with the glass*] There you are.

BROKER: Thank you.

> [*A beat between them.* ANNIE *goes away.*]

I'm not hearing from you as much.

CUTTER: I'm getting better service from the other brokers.

BROKER: My commission figures are down. The directors have
started to notice.

CUTTER: You've got my sympathy. [*Pause.*] What now?

BROKER: Look, I know you're not going to give me business out
of pity. [*Pause.*] If you want a holiday my firm owns a big

house in the Loire Valley. Swimming pool, house-keeper ... it's all laid on there. My firm'll pay for everything.

CUTTER: I hope you're not trying to corrupt me. [*to the others*] I'm not corruptible, am I?

NICK: No, you're already completely rotten.

BROKER: Stop playing with me, Graham.

CUTTER: I'm in charge of the conversation.

　　　　[*Pause.*]

BROKER: All right — but if you started giving me some of your turnover you might find a Lamborghini wrapped up outside your front door.

CUTTER: Splashing out, eh?

BROKER: My governor thinks I'm not spending enough on expenses. He thinks that's half my problem.

CUTTER: No, your problem is that when I pick up the phone looking for an offer it takes you too long to get me a taker. I'm left holding, and a new car won't change that.

BROKER: It's so ... fierce sometimes. Look, this isn't the right time to talk. I'll ring you.

CUTTER: You won't be able to — I'm taking your line out.

BROKER: Don't do that. Please.

CUTTER: You don't belong in this market.

　　　　[*A look between them. The* BROKER *goes.* JIMMY *is handing out the glasses of champagne.*]

IAN: What are we celebrating?

NICK: Don't be tiresome.

JIMMY: This occasion.

SARAH: Every night's an occasion. And lunchtime.

JIMMY: That's what I mean. Champagne's just for drinking.

NICK: You are learning, James, aren't you? You'll always be an oik but at least you'll be a refined one. [*Pause.*] Oh my God, I think Graham's attempting to be charming ...

　　　　[CUTTER *has resumed his conversation with* ANNIE.]

CUTTER: Right, as I was saying — this is the pound, OK? Sterling. [*He shows a pound coin in his palm.*] And these ... [*He takes two olives from the bar and places them in her palm.*] ... represent the dollar. And you're another bank. Now, suppose I think the pound is going down against the dollar. So I want to get rid of my pounds . . . [*He hands over the coin to her and takes the two olives from her.*] . . . in return for dollars. Now, suppose I'm right . . . there's bad money supply figures or Thatcher goes in for another eye operation — to make her see sense, ha ha . . . whatever — the pound is no longer worth as many . . . olives. I then sell my dollars back to you at a profit.

> [*He takes a bite of an olive. He gives her back the olives, one whole and one half-eaten. He takes back the pound coin. He indicates the piece of olive he's chewing.*]

This is my profit. And that's your loss. I win. You don't.

JIMMY: All most people know is how many pesetas they can get for their holidays.

SARAH: You're underestimating them.

NICK: Never overestimate the working class, that's what I say.

SARAH: Most of them are watching interest rates now. That's been the Thatch's big achievement — she's awakened their financial imagination.

NICK: What — this fashion for letting any old scumbag dive in for a share application? It's like the January sales.

SARAH: At least it's participation and not exclusion. Opportunities like that aren't to be shat on. People would be stupid not to.

IAN: It is not only desirable to want to own a BMW, it is your moral duty.

> [*We pick out* CUTTER *again.*]

CUTTER: It's just hot money looking for the most profitable place to go . . . from dollars into marks into Sterling and back again.

ANNIE: Still doesn't make any sense. All I know is every day it's like the gold rush has come. Euro-bond dealers, swaps specialists, futures traders . . . silk ties and plastic cards. But you know what's funny . . . you have to come underground to spend your money. It's like your prosperity can only be enjoyed out of sight of everybody else.

[JIMMY *approaches.*]

JIMMY: Well, I don't mind fucking flaunting it. Another bottle of pink glue please, Annie.

CUTTER: Wine bars can't keep all the unbearables below street level.

JIMMY: Eh?

ANNIE: The clientele.

JIMMY: The young, gifted and flash. Yeah, good, innit? Only people who used to gather in places like these were the absolutelies.

CUTTER: The what?

JIMMY: You know, cunts who say absolutely when all they really mean is yes.

ANNIE: I hope your mother loves you.

JIMMY: [*to* CUTTER] All right, ace. Come and help sort Nick the shit out.

[NICK *is arguing with* IAN.]

NICK: There's no decorum any more — the only gentlemen left are in merchant banking. Business should be arrangements with friends, not deals with other voices. It's got so we can't even go to lunch any more for fear of what the competition'll get up to in our absence.

IAN: Take it up with your trade union.

CUTTER: Don't you dare use that kind of language.

NICK: My father told me they used to hold inter-firm shooting competitions. Now no one knows how to shoot. Everybody just swears at each other and comes to work with gel in their hair. I don't care what you say, at least the old order had manners.

SARAH: They went home by tea-time, stinking of port, with their flies undone. At least we're efficient.

CUTTER: Anyway, there are new markets now, they need new skills. What hurts you is all the advantages that you grew up with don't mean shit with what we do. Everyone's there on merit. As it happens, your kind are in the minority now. Education doesn't make you a good dealer. It's gambling qualities. You don't learn them in Westminster and Kings. All they teach you there is how to take care of your own toothpaste. Everybody's got a chance now.

IAN: The Gnomes of Zurich have been replaced by the young spivs in shirtsleeves.

NICK: Well, whoever let you in has made a terrible mistake.

IAN: Who abandoned exchange controls in 1979?

NICK: The Tories.

IAN: Well then . . .

JIMMY: [*to* NICK] You and us are on the same side, really. We vote Conservative as well, you know. Look, let's have a toast. All pals together.

IAN: Toast what?

JIMMY: I don't know, think of something.

NICK: I suppose it might bring some elegance into the proceedings. [*Pause.*] I've got it! I think it's rather good, actually.

CUTTER: Well, get on with it.

NICK: What about . . . to the five marketeers.

JIMMY: What?

NICK: You know . . . all for one and one for all. I thought it was witty, actually.

IAN: Fucking hell.

SARAH: I'd rather toast bread.

CUTTER: No, come on, be fair. Suggested in good faith and with the best of intentions. We'll take up that toast, Nicholas, in the spirit it was intended. Solidarity across the social divide. No them and us any more.

IAN: You what?

CUTTER: Not in the dealing room, anyway.

JIMMY: It's not his fault he's an absolutely.

SARAH: A what?

IAN: I'm not doing that toast. It's stupid.

SARAH: [*handing him a glass of champagne*] Ian, don't be antisocial. You propose it, Nick. Your brainchild.

NICK: Oh . . . righto . . . to the . . . five marketeers!

ALL: The five marketeers!

[*They all drink except* IAN.]

JIMMY: Why aren't you drinking?

IAN: 'Cos I can't stand the taste of the bloody stuff. 'S'why I'm on Becks.

[He indicates a bottled beer.]

JIMMY: I don't like the taste much either but that ain't the point. You don't drink champagne because you like the taste, you drink it because . . . because you can.

IAN: That sort of logic leaves an even nastier taste in my mouth.

JIMMY: Fucking faintheart.

SARAH: What are you doing in FX anyway? It's like a vegetarian working in an abattoir.

IAN: Haven't you ever heard of infiltration? I'm planning a daring act of sabotage to bring about the downfall of international capitalism.

CUTTER: You enjoy the lifestyle too much.

IAN: Do I? You don't hear me going on about my top of the range E-reg. I don't live in a fifteenth-century converted inn just outside Maidstone.

CUTTER: Fourteenth-century, as it happens.

NICK: Poor old Ian's such a martyr.

CUTTER: You earn a lot of money. What d'you do with it, then?

IAN: That's a secret.

JIMMY: He needs corrupting.

NICK: How?

JIMMY: Let's get some bubbles into his bloodstream. Change his attitude.

NICK: What — pour some of the old posh glue down his throat?

[JIMMY advances on IAN.]

IAN: Keep away, you! If you make me drink that, you'll end up with Chateau vomit all over your three-hundred-pound Cerruti suit available from any branch of Woodhouse.

JIMMY: Get hold of him!

[CUTTER and NICK grab IAN by the arms and push him down into a chair. NICK restrains him by the legs as he struggles.]

NICK: D'you want to bite on a bullet or something?

[JIMMY *hands* SARAH IAN's *champagne glass.*]

SARAH: What's this for?

JIMMY: I'll hold his mouth open, you pour it in.

CUTTER: Any last requests?

IAN: Yeah — get cancer.

NICK: Just lie back and think of England. Well, not all of it — you can skip the Industrial North. I would.

[JIMMY *forces* IAN's *mouth open.* SARAH *looks on.*]

JIMMY: [*to* SARAH] Come on, then!

SARAH: But . . .

JIMMY: But what?

SARAH: It's cruel.

JIMMY: It's what? It's a laugh.

SARAH: What if he's sick?

JIMMY: That's what I mean. It's a laugh.

SARAH: That's terrible.

JIMMY: Look, are you a man or a mouse? Don't go all soppy. I thought you was one of us.

NICK: Come on, Sarah, don't be a wet blanket. It's only a bit of fun.

[SARAH *advances and stands over* IAN. *She inclines the glass to his mouth.*]

[*Blackout.*]

[IAN *and* JIMMY *sit together, drunk.*]

JIMMY: Dick Whittington came from up your way and look how he got on.

IAN: What are you saying?

JIMMY: Go for it, man. Don't keep sniping. You trade dollar/ yen. That's a good seat. Major turnover.

IAN: The first time I came into a dealing room I was delivering something.

JIMMY: Eh?

IAN: I was a despatch rider.

JIMMY: You was a greasy fucking biker?

IAN: That's how everyone in the dealing room looked at me. It was freezing outside, my face ached with the cold and all these young blokes were sitting in the warm with their clean shirts on, calling things out to each other. I thought, this is a job, you bastards? I could do this.

JIMMY: Only cunts ride motorbikes. Especially for a living. Always delivering to better places, never belonging to any of 'em.

IAN: I used to meet the other riders in Epping Forest on Sundays. Chelsea Bridge at night. Blokes from Scotland, Portsmouth . . . all over. London's where you have to come.

JIMMY: What's the matter . . . don't they talk to you now you ain't got shit all over your face?

IAN: There's not so much in common . . . I've kept my bike but I don't use it.

JIMMY: You're better off without them wankers . . . they all end up getting crushed under a bus sooner or later, anyway. You're the one who came in from the cold. Trouble with you is, you ain't quite got out your fucking leathers.

IAN: What about what you've left behind?

JIMMY: I ain't left it yet but when I do I ain't wearing a hair shirt for no one. Most of the kids on my estate are skag-heads, but look at all the credit cards I've got. [*showing him his wallet*] The bank's given me an in and I ain't letting go.

[SARAH *is getting ready to leave.* NICK *looks on.*]

NICK: I could go home with you.

SARAH: I don't fancy you.

NICK: So what? I'm horny and you've drunk too much. It's a perfect combination. Anyway, I don't want an office romance — just a fuck.

SARAH: You might not be any good at it. You might come too soon.

NICK: We could talk once it's over.

SARAH: What about?

NICK: Any old shit, really. After all, we've both been to university.

SARAH: Thanks for asking but I don't think I will.

NICK: Scared I'll tell?

SARAH: No. If you said anything out of turn I could just tell people you had a little willy.

NICK: What then — morals?

[*Pause.*]

SARAH: Sometimes I cry when I have an orgasm — I wouldn't want you to see that. There are pictures of me in my Holy Communion dress — I wouldn't want you to see them. The only thing I want you to know about me is how good I am on the corporate desk. I pick up pretty boys for sex, boys with little bums.

NICK: Charming.

SARAH: It's too dangerous with other dealers. [*Pause.*] Y'see — I've confessed three things already — you could use them against me. I'm so bloody porous, things leak out of me. Got to . . . keep the holes closed up. Got to stay tight.

NICK: What about a long snog in the doorway, then?

[CUTTER *is talking to* ANNIE, *who is clearing up the bar. He holds a small machine in his hand.*]

CUTTER: I just press this and I get a reading. The prices of the major currencies on the market that are being traded at the time. I look at this the way most people look at their watch. If I've got an overnight position on the pound I wake up in the dark to see how it's doing. I keep it on while I shave, it's with me at breakfast, I take it into restaurants. I don't listen to the radio or read news-papers — I just watch this. It's all I need to know. On Sunday nights it tells me what the market's doing in Asia. It's a Reuter's portable . . . the market never stops and I can't either.

ANNIE: It might stop you.

CUTTER: I can keep it up. Be a permanent fixture.

ANNIE: You reckon? [*Pause.*] No one who comes in here acts like there's anything permanent in what they have or what they do. No one drinks slowly or deliberately. They gulp and they grab and they spill too much so they have to buy some more. At first it seems like the excite-ment that comes with gold fever but then you see there's a panic there too.

CUTTER: That's why the markets are so volatile — they're made up of dealers who can't believe their luck and are wondering when it's going to run out.

ANNIE: So the markets are mostly emotional.

CUTTER: Yeah, fuck analysis. They don't run on that. It's the mood you're in. If the pound has had a bad day it's usually because some dealer had a row with his wife the night before. Gives him something to take it out on.

ANNIE: That's frightening.

CUTTER: That's market sentiment.

ANNIE: A sort of hysteria — that also finds its expression in conspicuous consumption.

CUTTER: Fucking hell — another one with a degree there's no job for.

ANNIE: All right then — a little test. How much have you spent tonight?

CUTTER: Haven't got a clue.

ANNIE: You see what I mean? Case proven.

CUTTER: Give me a receipt and I'll claim it on expenses. Case adjourned.

ANNIE: Why do the wrong sort of talents get rewarded?

CUTTER: The world's full of teachers.

ANNIE: I worked hard. Now it seems a waste. I can't get a post. I see people arranging to make each other richer down here and I make three pounds an hour, cleaning up after them . . . the bloody mess they make!

[*She is upset now.*]

CUTTER: You got something going with the broker?

ANNIE: Why? What's he said?

CUTTER: Nothing. Just the looks you were giving each other.

ANNIE: He told me he makes two hundred quid just by picking up the phone. That's how much he gave me.

CUTTER: What for?

[*She doesn't respond.*]

You fucked him for two hundred quid?

ANNIE: In your eyes nice girls don't do that sort of thing, I suppose?

CUTTER: I just think it's too cheap. You should have charged him more than that. [*Pause.*] Annie, is that still the going rate?

SCENE FOUR

A burglar alarm is ringing. Dim lights on CUTTER *sat down centre stage, holding a dead rabbit.* CAROL, CUTTER's *wife, emerges tentatively, shining a torch and holding a pair of scissors, as if in defence. The torch picks out* CUTTER.

CUTTER: I forgot my keys.

CAROL: How do I turn this bloody thing off!

CUTTER: The switch in the cupboard.

> [CAROL *disappears momentarily. The burglar alarm stops ringing.* CAROL *returns.*]

CAROL: Don't know why you had it installed in the first place.

CUTTER: We've got a lot to protect, that's why. Thieves'd have a field day.

CAROL: I thought one of the ideas of moving down here was that there wouldn't be any trouble like that. You said the only crime they had down here was sheep-rustling.

CUTTER: Well, if you think there's nothing to worry about, why were you holding those scissors like a maniac?

CAROL: I wasn't.

CUTTER: Well, you weren't altering curtains.

CAROL: [*indicating the rabbit*] Who's your friend?

CUTTER: I wanted to see if the traps worked that I set.

CAROL: [*sarcastic*] That survival course was money well spent, then?

CUTTER: They teach you how to skin 'em as well. Get a knife out the kitchen — I'll show you.

CAROL: No thanks.

CUTTER: The next one's on avoiding capture — y'know, dog evasion techniques and all that. Come in handy the next time you're hunting for me.

CAROL: Pretending to escape from things at your age.

CUTTER: That's the whole point of it — escapism.

CAROL: Did you win today?

CUTTER: Why d'you think I'm late?

CAROL: I don't know. If you win, you celebrate. If you lose, you need consolation. Either way, you end up drinking champagne.

CUTTER: I'm a player. That's why we live like this. When the dealing's finished I need a release.

CAROL: When we first moved here I thought this place might be haunted. A six-hundred-year-old converted inn — I thought I might see a headless highwayman or a moaning pirate. But the only thing that appears at night and upsets me is you. And funnily enough, I'm the one who wanders round this house like a ghost, like a lost soul.

CUTTER: You ought to find yourself a hobby.

CAROL: What am I supposed to do — go to point-to-points in the Range Rover? I can't even bloody drive!

CUTTER: Make friends with the neighbours, then.

CAROL: The only neighbours we've got are either farmers or people who work in advertising. Anyway, the nearest one's a quarter of a mile away. You wanted splendid isolation, remember?

CUTTER: How dare you say you're unhappy here — this is one of the most beautiful parts of Kent, this is the bloody garden of England. Our village green is where the first game of cricket was ever played — did you know that? This is the real thing, this — there's nothing mock about any of it.

CAROL: I keep banging my head on the oak beams. [*Pause.*] We used to have more going for us than just your achievements.

CUTTER: You couldn't wait to escape from where we came from. You bring clothes home from Brown's now. Don't say you haven't enjoyed our . . . progress.

CAROL: But it's all happened so fast. I'd only just stopped congratulating myself on us getting a semi in Eltham.

CUTTER: Anyone can be suburban.

CAROL: I'm a working-class girl and I don't need to work any more. I'm confused. This doesn't seem like a life, Graham, it's more like a holiday I want to come home from.

CUTTER: In the past, down here was the only holiday your mum and dad ever got. Hop-picking. All they had to escape to . . . we own it. We live it.

[CAROL *sits down beside him.*]

CAROL: You made it sound like we'd found something idyllic. At first I believed you.

CUTTER: We're sitting on our own land.

CAROL: We used to sit in the park and be happy.
[*She lies across him, her head resting on his thighs.*]
Get us a 99 from the ice cream van.

CUTTER: Queueing up, then carrying it back feeling like a twat. What else?

CAROL: Blades of grass.

CUTTER: Sticking them in your ear, annoying you. What else?

CAROL: The dogs used to come and sniff your crotch.

CUTTER: So did you.

CAROL: Don't be disgusting.

CUTTER: What else?

CAROL: The top twenty. Guessing what would be number one. Turning up the ones we liked.

CUTTER: My change used to fall out of my pocket.

CAROL: Trust you to remember money.

CUTTER: What else?

CAROL: For Christ's sake stop asking what else!

CUTTER: I need to be reminded.

CAROL: I remember everything.

CUTTER: Tell me.

CAROL: You try. You bloody well try.

CUTTER: You're better at remembering than me.

CAROL: Why d'you think that is?

CUTTER: I don't know.

CAROL: I like the past. How we used to be was better than this.

CUTTER: Maybe.

CAROL: Say so.

CUTTER: Eh?

CAROL: Say things were better! I want to hear you say it.

CUTTER: No! I'll never fucking say it! You have to change, you have to progress. You just can't, that's all. You're wearing a three-hundred-pound jumper there and you look like shit in it! You're supposed to look different, you're supposed to look expensive.

CAROL: I thought you always liked how I looked. [*Pause.*] We're wearing money, that's all. We haven't learned to make it natural. We never will. [*Pause.*] Let's take all this designer shit off. Let's just fuck each other in the grass.

CUTTER: You know what happened last time. And the time before that.

CAROL: It might be more successful outdoors. More exciting.

CUTTER: You make it sound like a treatment.

CAROL: It might have to come to that.

CUTTER: Never.

CAROL: Come on, then, nothing on. Just sweating.

CUTTER: Back to nature now, eh? I thought you didn't like the country.

CAROL: I just want us to do something simple together! Roll around like we were in the park!

CUTTER: I wasn't the cable dealer in the park!

CAROL: Forget about your job for once. It's the stress that's causing it.

CUTTER: I'm not impotent.
[*Pause.*]

CAROL: What's wrong with me, then?

CUTTER: The women in the dealing room and the other banks always look so good. We've got dealing in common. Why aren't you . . . exciting like them? I see your face and it's what's been, not what's going on. I'm sorry.
[*Pause.*]

CAROL: I see. You don't want to let go of the past but you can't face getting on top of it and fucking it. Is that right? [*Pause.*] You think you've . . . grown into something, don't you? You've just shrunk, shrivelled. You kill everything. When the Predictor turned pink you said we should wait. And that's all I've done . . . sat in our real estate, waiting for you to let me have the only thing I really wanted.

CUTTER: It's late.

CAROL: And the market'll be open again soon, eh?

SCENE FIVE

The dealing room. JIMMY, NICK, SARAH *and* IAN *are in attendance.* JULIE *enters.*

JULIE: [*to* JIMMY] The showroom's bringing your car round.

JIMMY: Oh blinding! Who the fuck needs Father Christmas when you've got a fourteen grand car allowance?

JULIE: I wouldn't know about that.

JIMMY: No, course not. [*Pause.*] You can have a ride in it if you like.

JULIE: Might as well — be the nearest thing you ever get to an act of charity.

JIMMY: I wasn't sure whether to have the 924 or the 944. I mean, what d'you get for paying an extra few grand — an ejector seat? A young man needs advice about this sort of thing. I'm going down to wait for it.

SARAH: [*reacting to something that's just come up on the screen*] Fuck.

NICK: Oh my God — it's happening.

JIMMY: What's happening?

IAN: The end of the fourteen grand car allowance as we know it. And more. Much more. On the Reuter's screen — look.

JULIE: [*reading it off*] "Goldman Lovett believed to be having discussions with the Office of Fair Trading on airline finance deal. A Bank of England spokesman said unless significant progress was made they could not rule out the possibility of suspension of Goldman Lovett's banking licence."

JIMMY: They can't do that! Nobbled — us?

SARAH: They can and it doesn't bear thinking about.

NICK: I don't feel very well — has anyone got any Anadin?

JULIE: If they suspend our banking licence, what then?

SARAH: We'd have to close down.

JULIE: What — like a factory?

IAN: Exactly.

SARAH: For a year, anyway.

NICK: I wonder what it's like to be made redundant.

IAN: Ask the gilts dealers at Salomon and Chemical — they soon found out a bull market doesn't last forever.

JIMMY: Fuck off, you! My car'll have to stay in the showroom. It's got a sixteen-valve engine. It's not fair.

NICK: But they can't treat us like car workers — can they?

SARAH: They'd have no choice. The bank'd have to switch its operations to Frankfurt for the time being.

JIMMY: Wouldn't they take us with 'em?

SARAH: Can you speak German?

IAN: Only German he knows is BMW.

NICK: This isn't bloody funny! Our bloody epitaphs have just appeared on the screen and you're bloody laughing. [*Pause.*] After the Crash I thought we could survive anything.

JIMMY: Anyway, we wouldn't have to speak Kraut in Germany, would we?

JULIE: I don't see what you're all so worried about. You're all dealers — you can get jobs in other banks. Midland or Nat West.

JIMMY: What — and have to pay the proper tax? Are you fucking sure?

SARAH: [*to* JULIE] We're on a dual contract here — half our money's paid in New York. Besides which, British banks don't pay as much commission.

JULIE: What about the Japanese?

NICK: Oxbridge graduates only, my dear.

JULIE: You'll be all right, then.

NICK: Yes, I was at Oxford.

IAN: Oxford Polytechnic.

NICK: Semantics!

JIMMY: Point is, Julie, we're cracking away here. If they have to fuck off to Frankfurt, that's no good to me — I've got expensive tastes.

NICK: It's bloody inconvenient — all over some poxy British planes.

JIMMY: What we need is Maggie to step in and do a Westland.
[JULIE *exits.* CUTTER *appears.*]
You seen this, Graham? [*indicating the screen*] They won't suspend our banking licence, will they?

CUTTER: It's a bit like the nuclear threat. All right as a deterrent but unthinkable to use it.

JIMMY: He's so cool.

IAN: But he's wrong. This is suspension, not total withdrawal. Not irreversible, like letting a Cruise missile go.

CUTTER: True. Perhaps we're going to be made a lesson of.

IAN: Probity in the City.

JIMMY: But they couldn't go ahead — it'd still be a disaster, wouldn't it?

SARAH: Only a limited one.

NICK: A sort of deliberate financial Chernobyl.

IAN: That's in bad taste.

NICK: Fuck taste — my career's at stake!

CUTTER: Let's not get hysterical. I really think they'll leave well alone . . . banking's too much of a house of cards. We'll be all right.

IAN: [*to* NICK] Internal line.

[NICK *picks up the phone.*]

NICK: Charlie? Oh. OK.

[*He puts the phone down.*]

Well, that's that.

SARAH: That's what?

NICK: South's coming down to make an announcement.

SARAH: Must be bad news about something.

NICK: It's oblivion. I know it is. We're all fucking doomed.

IAN: Nomura's taking us over.

JIMMY: ⎫
NICK: ⎭ Where d'you hear that?

IAN: I made it up.

JIMMY: ⎫
NICK: ⎭ Cunt!

[CROSS *arrives with* SOUTH.]

CROSS: If I could have your attention, please — Mr. South just wants to have a few words with you all.

SOUTH: Thank you, Charlie.[*Pause; a general address*] Have you had a good day?

JIMMY: I won sixty grand.

SOUTH: That's what I like to hear. How did cable go?

CUTTER: Not too well.

SOUTH: I'm sure you'll be ahead at the end of the week. [*Pause; generally*] I'm also sure that today's work isn't the only kind of speculation that's been going on in here. Which is not how it should be and I've come to put it right. Because you're the most important people in this bank, its biggest breadwinners and what you do is the reason we came to London, the reason we stay.

JIMMY: [*to* NICK]This sounds hopeful.

SOUTH: Yes, son, and I come with the happy announcement that the Director General of Fair Trading has dropped his request for us to change our loan requirements. The airline will still get its planes but the order will go to Seattle. It's business as usual.

> [*This is greeted by applause and general delight.*]

IAN: But they're supposed to be a quango. Independent.

SOUTH: A word was had into their independent ear. The misconception about unfair competition has now been . . . clarified.

JIMMY: She's done a Westland!

SOUTH: Trade relations were a consideration. Besides, the regulators of the City know they're not in a position to carry out any threats. Otherwise it would be a signal that the Authorities were no longer concerned to keep London as a world financial centre. It wants, it needs, the limelight so it can't complain about the acts. The only reason Johnson Matthey was rescued was to keep London at the forefront of the gold market.

NICK: I love the ingenuity of free enterprise.

CROSS: So how's this one going to come out, Mr. South?

SOUTH: The Fed and the Bank of England are going to stitch up a compromise — a reciprocity deal. One of the UK clearing banks is going to get an investment arm in the States. They'll get eaten alive but we go on, and having been the bearer of glad tidings I want to bring a note of caution in. Charlie?

> [*He invites* CROSS *to address them.*]

CROSS: Watch out for those fucking Japanese.

SOUTH: Latest figures show that turnover in their own market is almost as high as New York's. They're getting busier here but I've got every faith in my dealers and I go back to what I said earlier — you're our most valuable assets . . . Britain's golden children.

JIMMY: I wish my old probation officer could hear this.

SOUTH: Before I go, a little story that might interest you . . . during the last Labour administration, when there was a serious speculative run on the pound, Prime Minister Callaghan complained, "But there used to be a little man at the Bank of England who dealt with this sort of thing."

[*Laughter.* SOUTH *exits.*]

CROSS: The market's come a long way since it upset Callaghan.

IAN: Speculation's respectable now.

SARAH: And this Bank's looking impregnable.

NICK: We're probably always going to be safe, aren't we?

CUTTER: Why not — what rules there are just don't apply to us. The free market's never been so free.

JIMMY: We're the untouchables! [*to* CUTTER] And you can take money off anyone in the world . . . more Japs in London won't make any difference.

NICK: I hear their conditions of employment are rather severe. If you don't make a profit at the end of the year you have to commit harakiri.

IAN: Different here — other people put the knife into you when things aren't going well.

[JULIE *appears.*]

JULIE: It's here.

JIMMY: My keys await me.

[*He starts to go.*]

NICK: This I must see.

IAN: I bet he stalls it.

SARAH: Does it come with the furry dice and the George Benson tapes?

JIMMY: Coming, Graham?

CUTTER: I can watch you tearing round the City in it from up here.

JIMMY: I'll be coming in for a pit stop.

CUTTER: I'll check it out then.

> [JIMMY *goes, followed by the others.* JULIE *looks on.*]

JULIE: I don't know . . . a football hooligan on a footballer's wages.

> [JULIE *goes to join the others.* CROSS *and* CUTTER *are alone.*]

CROSS: I remember that was you a few years ago . . . a little Jack the lad on Australian dollar.

CUTTER: And you were the cable dealer.

CROSS: Progress, eh?

CUTTER: What's it like to watch, Charlie?

CROSS: You sound almost envious.

CUTTER: I'm interested to know what my future might be like.

CROSS: Well, for a start, it's good to go home at five o'clock because you can see the sense of going home. And your kids have drawings they want to show you.

CUTTER: You've kept everything intact. It's harder to do that now.

CROSS: I love my survival. [*Pause.*] Have you got any investments, Graham, your money in futures or bonds?

CUTTER: Why d'you ask that all of a sudden?

CROSS: I want to know that you're looking after yourself.

CUTTER: What I make I spend.

CROSS: Nothing tied up in property?

CUTTER: Just the coach-house.

CROSS: My cable dealer's still a financial illiterate — I don't believe it.

CUTTER: You've hedged your bets all over the place, I suppose?

CROSS: I think you should too. In fact I'm telling you.

CUTTER: I've never been cautious — you know that. Never had cause.

CROSS: One of the things about being Chief Dealer is I look everywhere now, not just in front of a Reuter's display. It means you get political. Get political, Graham.

> [*He goes.* CUTTER *is left alone momentarily.* SARAH *appears.*]

SARAH: Jimmy's just bought a bottle of Louis Roederer to launch the car with. "Bless this 924 and all who pose in her." Ian tried to let one of the tyres down. Nick's hoping he'll get done for speeding. I just left him trying to attract a police car's attention. Julie looks a bit embarrassed by it all. [*Pause.*] It's a red one, of course. Easy to sniff out what a vulgar little shit he is but no one's discreet when they're twenty-two, are they? [*Pause.*] Something wrong, Graham?

CUTTER: My wife's fucked off.

SARAH: I'm sorry.

CUTTER: I'll have to get a guard dog. [*Pause.*] I'm not as careless as Charlie thinks.

SARAH: Seems odd to think about anyone who'd like me enough to want to marry me.

> [CUTTER *leans over and vomits.*]

CUTTER: Shit!

SARAH: Oh Jesus, Graham — are you all right?

CUTTER: Just go and get the others back. Tell them the money supply figures'll be out soon. I'll need some calls. [*Pause.*] Go on!

> [SARAH *goes.* CUTTER *picks up the phone.*]

Looking for a price in forty quid. Mine!

> [*He makes another call.*]

Looking for a price in forty quid. Mine!

> [*Another call.*]

Looking for a price in twenty quid. Mine!

> [*The others return.*]

How is it?

JIMMY: It's fierce, man. It roars.

NICK: What he means is, he's over-revving it.

JIMMY: Have you heard those car horns that play a tune? I'm getting one installed.

IAN: What tune?

JIMMY: 'I'm forever blowing bubbles.'

IAN: A fair old Porsche for a fair day's work.

JIMMY: That's still half the trouble in this country — not enough people have got the incentive to get to become like us.

IAN: Thank fuck.

SARAH: Don't worry — it's in the twenty-five year plan. They're working on it.

CUTTER: Come on — get ready for this announcement.

JIMMY: How soon?

CUTTER: Three minutes.

IAN: What's the forecast?

CUTTER: One and a half per cent. That's a lot better than last month.

NICK: So you've got into a position on it?

CUTTER: A hundred quid.

NICK: Your funeral.

CUTTER: I'm the fucking cable dealer.

[CROSS *appears.*]

CROSS: [*to* CUTTER] Pulling rank again?

IAN: Graham's giving the Chancellor the benefit of the doubt about M3.

CROSS: How?

NICK: He's bought a hundred million quids' worth in advance of the announcement.

CUTTER: I'm only looking to pick up a quick fifty or sixty points. The market still responds to good news, doesn't it?

CROSS: What's happening to the price?

CUTTER: It hasn't moved much yet.

CROSS: That's because the dealers of the other banks are going in flat. They're not making any bets.

NICK: They don't share Graham's confidence.

CUTTER: So you're telling me the Government doesn't have an anti-inflation policy any more? That's not what the Governor of the fucking Bank of England said yesterday!

CROSS: Cut out, Graham.

CUTTER: No way.

CROSS: Get rid of your Sterling.

CUTTER: What for? The price isn't going down. It's staying at my level.

JIMMY: Figures out any second now!

[*They wait, eyes glued to the screens or listening intently to anything that comes out of the brokers' boxes.*]

IAN: [*announcing*] Up three and a half!

CUTTER: What?

IAN: Up three and a half per cent!

CUTTER: But the forecast was only one and a half!

CROSS: It's busted its target again.

NICK: Chancellor speak with forked tongue.

CUTTER: Calls please, quickly!

[*The others pick up their phones.*]

NICK: What are you calling cable?

IAN: Can I have a spot for cable?

JIMMY: Cable quote!

CUTTER: [*picking up his phone*] If you're looking for an offer you've got it!

CROSS: What d'you pay?

CUTTER: Eighty-five.

NICK: Seventy-five/eighty!

CUTTER: Shit. Yours.

NICK: [*down the phone*] Twenty-five yours.

JIMMY: Seventy-one to six!

CUTTER: That's even lower.

CROSS: Take it at a loss.

CUTTER: Yours!

JIMMY: Twenty-five given! [*off the phone*] Given away, more like.

NICK: Fifty-five/sixty!

CUTTER: Fucking hell!

NICK: Twenty-five yours!

JIMMY: Fifty-one to six! [*down the phone*] Twenty-five yours!

IAN: Forty-three/fifty.

NICK: Forty/forty-five.

CUTTER: I'm taking a bashing.

CROSS: That's enough calls.

[*A general air of embarrassment at* CUTTER*'s disenchantment. Heads down, the rest fill in dealing slips.*]

JIMMY: [*generally*] I suppose what we need now is a news alert to say Reagan's had a heart attack. Last time there was a scare like that the dollar went down a cent till we found out it wasn't Reagan having trouble with his ticker, it was Lonnie Donnegan.

[*The amusement of the rest at this loosens things somewhat.*]

CUTTER: [*still preoccupied with his loss*] But I don't understand it, the pound's been so strong lately — all the attention's been on the dollar. Every announcement that's come out, the market's decided was good for Sterling. Growth up, unemployment down. An announcement like that shouldn't have upset the market — I mean, the economy's basically sound.

NICK: Listen to him — he thinks he's an analyst.

CROSS: At least analysts know there's no such thing as monetarism any more.

NICK: Yes, the Government's done a complete U-turn to Keynes and inflation but the economy's basically sound.

IAN: Trumpton's got a bigger manufacturing industry than this country but the economy's basically sound.

NICK: There's been a consumer boom of Sonys and Audis bought with Barclaycard but the economy's basically sound.

IAN: We've just about turned into an offshore banking island, a bigger version of the Isle of Man . . .

IAN: ⎫
NICK: ⎬ But the economy's basically sound!

[JULIE *appears with McDonald's hamburgers for everybody.*]

JULIE: What were the figures like?

CUTTER: I was over-optimistic.

SARAH: Nothing wrong with optimism.

IAN: It's easy to be optimistic about Great Britain Limited when you've got a glass of champagne in your hand. And he's had a whole vineyard's worth over the years.

CUTTER: Just shut it!

IAN: What's your problem?

CUTTER: What do you believe in — that nothing works? What sort of fucking belief is that? Trouble with people like you is you think turning up your nose is an act of imagination. I'm not going to change what I think just because something's gone wrong. You can't rebuild an economy without some sacrifices. Convictions are what count and I've got the courage of mine. You and your kind carry out market research before you know what you should think — blankets and benefits for everyone. That's weakness and there's no respect for it, no success in it.

NICK: You've lost a few quid so we're taking the piss — where's your sense of humour?

CROSS: He left it behind on his ego trip.

JIMMY: I know the figures were bad but we're still on the road to recovery, ain't we? I mean, compared to the States we're doing all right. Ain't we?

[*Pause.*]

CROSS: You never bank on your country, Jimmy, till you know what the rest of the market's doing. Otherwise it's a mug's game.

JIMMY: He just did.

CUTTER: I'll still have the best figures in the room at the end of the week. Like I always do.

JIMMY: How old are you now, Graham?

END OF ACT ONE

ACT TWO

SCENE ONE

A desk representing an older-style office. A middle-aged man, wearing a factory overall/apron, shirt and tie beneath, works on the frame of an umbrella. He is MR. MILLAR, SARAH'*s father. He gets up to greet her as she enters.*

SARAH: Congratulations, Dad!

MILLAR: [*indicating the umbrella*] The beginning of export orders everywhere!

SARAH: Anywhere it rains a lot.

MILLAR: Anywhere they appreciate craft a lot. And Germany'll do for starters.

SARAH: Show me.

MILLAR: I've shown you before.

SARAH: You know you love to.

MILLAR: [*holding out the umbrella*] You carve out slots for the handspring and topspring. There and there.

SARAH: They're just bits of wire.

MILLAR: Not when we've finished with them. [*Pause.*] Stoppers in place and the runners, look, I have eight slots for the ribs to go in. Eight ribs make the frame. You won't see these having to be fastened with a nasty bit of cloth and a clip. There's some order samples in that box if you want to have a look.

SARAH: You should branch out into luggage, Dad.

MILLAR: We're specialists, Sarah, not a department store. These are already on sale in a noted Jermyn St. outfitters, I'll have you know.

SARAH: I'm so pleased it's going well. I know it was a big decision to start this up.

MILLAR: I had your encouragement. Anyway, it wasn't hard to run away from personnel management. There's real satisfaction here. Not just the craft but knowing you can make a go of something. This German order's proof of the pudding.

SARAH: It's a good time for the little man with big ideas.

MILLAR: Medium-sized ones, anyway. [*Pause.*] I'm sure there's a ready market at that bank of yours, Sarah. It's an essential accessory for the City gent. Hand-made umbrellas are a mark of distinction — don't they want to walk to work with distinction? Sticks made of root ash or polished hickory and cherry.

SARAH: I've already told you, Dad — they're not the bowler and briefcase brigade. When it rains they jump into a cab.

MILLAR: That's a nasty American habit.

SARAH: Oh, they've got lots of those.

MILLAR: Well, at least the Germans appreciate us. [*Pause.*] So it's payment in Deutschmarks if you please.

SARAH: You wanted advice.

MILLAR: I certainly do. I don't want to get caught in a currency fluctuation. And well . . . I'm still thinking in pounds, shillings and pence.

SARAH: You need a finance director.

MILLAR: Finance director? First things first. I'm doing all I can to try and find a tipper.

SARAH: A what?

MILLAR: Someone who can hand-sew the covers on. I don't like sending out for the work to be done.

SARAH: It'd keep costs down, I suppose.

MILLAR: It's the quality I want to guarantee. [*Pause.*] Anyway, I've got a daughter who's a currency expert. So start advising . . .

SARAH: When's the payment due?

MILLAR: About a month from now.

SARAH: You could hedge by selling forward — arrange to take delivery in a month's time at today's rate. But it's not really worth it as the mark won't soften against the pound.

MILLAR: What else?

SARAH: Take out an option to sell marks, let the option lapse and then sell spot. It's another way of hedging, but the upside potential is so much better where the mark's concerned. [*Pause.*] You'd cash in if it rose.

MILLAR: Sounds wonderful.

SARAH: Only drawback is, there's a premium.

MILLAR: I've got enough costs to confront as it is.
> [*Pause.*]
SARAH: Why not do nothing?
MILLAR: What d'you mean?
SARAH: Just take the Deutschmarks in a month's time at the market rate. Just wait.
MILLAR: Will I lose out doing that?
SARAH: Course not — the market forecast is for the mark to go up against Sterling. Besides, that's almost traditional.
MILLAR: But that sounds like speculation. I don't want to be on the receiving end of a . . . a bear market. Like all those people did in October.
SARAH: That was different. Equity prices can only go up or down. With currencies, any sign of trouble and you move into another.
MILLAR: And there'll be no trouble with the mark, will there?
SARAH: Not with an economy like theirs. Not inside a month.
MILLAR: Well, I don't have great faith in the markets but I've got faith in you.
> [*He produces a bottle of drink and two cups.*]
> So it's not too soon to celebrate?
SARAH: Definitely not. What's German for umbrellas?
MILLAR: Regenschirmen.
SARAH: Let's hope they go down there as well as they go up.
MILLAR: To Regenschirmen.
> [*They drink to it.*]
> Do they appreciate you at that bank of yours?
SARAH: I hope so.
MILLAR: They didn't think you'd last long, did they?
SARAH: Only because I cried the first time someone swore at me.
MILLAR: Men shouldn't swear at women.
SARAH: That was a long time ago.
MILLAR: They've stopped, then?
SARAH: Course not — it's just that now I can shout bollocks as loudly as the rest of them. [*Pause.*] You have to develop another skin, Dad, so you don't expose yourself to anything — the other dealers, the way they're behaving, the names they call you — dead to it all. You just keep

picking up the phone and all you feel is anger or elation
— a bad trade or a good one.

MILLAR: Sounds dreadful.

SARAH: [*a little wryly*] I've always been career-minded . . . now
I've succeeded.

MILLAR: You could always come and work here — we'd have a
small family business then.

SARAH: No — I can hack it.

SCENE TWO

The races at Ascot. SOUTH, *installed in the Bank's box, is
dressed in top hat and tails. He is watching the proceedings
through binoculars. He is duly joined by* CROSS, *similarly
attired.*

SOUTH: I feel ridiculous, dressed like this.

CROSS: It's the done thing, Mr. South. You'd look out of place
otherwise. It's one of the most important social events
in the calendar.

SOUTH: So any time something significant takes place in this
country you have to wear clothes you normally wouldn't
be seen dead in.

CROSS: It's tradition.

SOUTH: Your hat doesn't fit you right.

CROSS: It's all they had. [*Pause.*] There's a lot of titled people
here.

SOUTH: [*sardonic*] The Duke and Duchess of Cucumber, you
mean? The Earl of Auchtermuchty?

CROSS: They're all well-connected.

SOUTH: I'm well-connected, they just own their own costumes.
But then again, that's probably why you're impressed.

CROSS: You don't think they've still got influence in this country, power?

SOUTH: They've got privilege but access to the members'
enclosure isn't power. Real power's not conferred, it's
taken. In the States, the men running Exxon grew up in
tenements. They won their positions, they didn't inherit

them. Capitalism's for everyone — not just the people whose top hats are custom-made. That's a lesson this country's learning. [*Pause.*] I was looking at the overall dealing figures for the past two weeks — what's going on?

CROSS: I know there's been more ebb than flow.

SOUTH: You talk like it's seasonal.

CROSS: I'll give the dealers a pep-talk. One in particular.

SOUTH: I may talk bullish but October taught us all a lesson in fragility. I'm watching very carefully — everything.

> [JIMMY *appears. He too is wearing the traditional Ascot garb, as are the other dealers, who enter later.*]

Enjoying yourself, son?

JIMMY: Blinding. Here I am in the members' enclosure with my lords, ladies and gentlemen.

SOUTH: Impressed?

JIMMY: I've already got a lot in common with this crowd.

SOUTH: What's that?

JIMMY: I don't like horseracing much either.

> [SOUTH *laughs.*]

I'm not a social climber, Mr. South. I don't want to go to the opera. I still wanna play football on Sunday mornings for my club — but I wanna turn up in a Roller.

SOUTH: You don't want to leave your class, you just want to lord it over them.

JIMMY: They're queueing up at the tote. I'm here.

SOUTH: You remind me of the Artful Dodger.

JIMMY: The Artful Dodger was a loser. Oliver ended up living in the big house.

SOUTH: That was his birthright.

JIMMY: I don't need one of those.

SOUTH: [*to* CROSS] He's promising.

CROSS: You're due for the presentation of the Cup now, Mr. South. To the winning jockey.

SOUTH: What was the name of the horse again?

CROSS: Fallen Idol.

SOUTH: Owned by the Queen . . . how about that? Does that mean she gets the prize money we put up?

CROSS: Well . . . yes.

SOUTH: Our bank sponsors a race and the British monarchy gets the benefit. I like the idea of that. Can I hand it over to her in person?

CROSS: That's not done.

SOUTH: [*teasingly*] Tradition?

CROSS: Protocol. She hasn't arrived yet, anyway.

SOUTH: Remind me of the trainer's name again . . . Sir something?

CROSS: Sir Henry.

SOUTH: Here, you can borrow my binoculars . . . get a bird's eye view of me handing out the gifts to the natives.

[*He goes.*]

CROSS: I hope you're behaving.

JIMMY: I saw some Henrietta. She was talking like she had toffee in her mouth. She was a bit freckly but I pulled her. I thought I might as well. I've been snogging with her up against the rails.

CROSS: This is supposed to be a day out on the Bank, not pillage and plunder.

JIMMY: She lives on her father's estate. What a coincidence I said — I live on an estate as well.

CROSS: Where is she now?

JIMMY: Fuck knows. Running in the two-thirty probably.

[SARAH *emerges, taking pictures with a camera.*]

Oi, capture me for posterity!

SARAH: Your vulgarity's not unique here, Jimmy — I've just seen a woman wearing a hat in the shape of a toilet.

JIMMY: You know the working class, Sarah — give 'em a bit of money and it goes to their heads. In the shape of a toilet.

[*He exits.*]

CROSS: Where are the others?

SARAH: Nick's met some old friends. They're braying like donkeys. Graham's drinking too much.

CROSS: Worried about him?

SARAH: That's the maternal side of me coming out.

CROSS: What's there to worry about, Sarah?

SARAH: Nothing. He just shouldn't be drinking.

CROSS: You sound like a doctor.

SARAH: Do I?

CROSS: Something else is going on.

SARAH: I don't know anything.

CROSS: Yes you do. Anything that's affecting his dealing, Sarah, I wanna hear about it. Dying mother, cat run over, premature ejaculation . . . if you know his problem, Sarah, tell me.

SARAH: Ask him yourself.

CROSS: I doubt if I'll get anything out of him.

SARAH: But you think you can out of me.

CROSS: Dealers with problems are not at their best . . . there's usually money at stake. The Bank's. And what's the most important thing, Sarah?

SARAH: I don't know.

CROSS: Yes you do! You don't lose money for the Bank . . . that comes before everything . . . so if you want to be pro-fessional instead of emotional you won't protect him and fuck the Bank up, will you? Well?
> [*No response.*]
> You've got a reputation for being a no-nonsense FX trader, Sarah . . . I'm not seeing it. [*Pause.*] We're all affected.
> [*Pause.*]

SARAH: I took him to hospital. They gave me his clothes to hold in a plastic bag while they held his mouth open and pushed a rubber tube into his stomach. They were checking for internal bleeding.
> [JIMMY *emerges, having been eavesdropping.*]

JIMMY: That explains a bit.

SARAH: Shit.

JIMMY: Most people slump in front of the telly after a hard day at the office; they don't end up in a casualty department.

SARAH: I'm going to watch the next race.

JIMMY: Pick us the winner, Sarah.
> [SARAH *exits.*]

CROSS: You had no business listening.

JIMMY: We're all affected. [*Pause.*] You've been on to him for a while, haven't you? Why haven't you done anything?

CROSS: Who do you think you are?

JIMMY: The contender.

CROSS: We've only just stopped sending you out for sandwiches. Anyway, we're talking about a rough patch, not retirement.

JIMMY: Benefit of the doubt, eh?

CROSS: Why not? He deserves it — he's been a dealer longer than anyone. I gave him his apprenticeship.

JIMMY: You'll be presenting him with a gold watch next.

CROSS: He's never given me cause for complaint. He's always been the best player in the room.

JIMMY: Time serving ain't on any more, Charlie. Did you hear what happened on the floor of the Chicago Futures Exchange . . . ? A trader died of a heart attack. Actually in the pit itself . . . he was twenty-nine. The next day they were going to hold a two minutes' silence for him — a mark of respect. Then they decided they couldn't give him two minutes . . . it would disrupt the markets too much. So they agreed on a minute . . . and the traders stopped and stood there in silence. But some had been in the middle of buying and selling contracts; they began to worry about losing out on the orders they had to execute . . . others beating them to it once the minute was up. So they started to fidget — one or two hand signals started up, someone protested, someone got punched and in a few seconds trading started up on the floor again — they were shouting and screaming and waving their order slips. They remembered the dead trader for twenty-three seconds. It's all they could give.

CROSS: That's just fucking indecent.

JIMMY: It ain't work any more, it's fanaticism. My turn now, Charlie. I'm not just a cheeky chappie.

CROSS: Dealing's about relationships as well, son.

JIMMY: What — loyalty? [*Pause.*] I know this might sound like a silly question but I thought dealing was mainly about beating other dealers. You know, your gain is their loss. Ain't it?

CROSS: Other banks, not your own team.

JIMMY: I was in a pub where I live the other week and there was a row. Two kids about some girl. They were squaring up. One put up his fists ready to go in. The other one just took out a Stanley and cut him to pieces. The loser was taken out of the pub with half his face hanging off. I hoped he learnt something. I did. Anything goes.

CROSS: In a high street on a Friday night but not in my section.

JIMMY: Watch out, Charlie — your management's getting out of date.

> [JIMMY *and* CROSS *exit.* IAN *enters, carrying a picnic hamper. He is not wearing hat and tails, just an ordinary suit. He opens the hamper and starts checking the contents.*]

IAN: Pâté with quails' eggs . . . asparagus in stem ginger . . . fresh smoked salmon with dill . . .

> [SARAH *appears.*]

SARAH: What are you doing?

IAN: Will your stomach take food your brain has never heard of? [*Pause.*] You see that tick-tack man over there? He's signalling the prices of the horses with his hands. What's the difference between him and us?

SARAH: About ninety grand a year.

IAN: Spot on.

> [SARAH *starts laying out the food from the hamper.*]

SARAH: Isn't it a shame about poor people?

IAN: What?

SARAH: That's about all your hand-wringing amounts to.

IAN: I'm no fucking liberal.

SARAH: Might as well be. You're on the inside looking in — doesn't give much moral weight to your argument. It's just plain old-fashioned guilt.

IAN: I can lend you some if you're running short.

SARAH: I haven't done anything.

IAN: I watch you a lot, Sarah. I could tell you what clothes you've been wearing any day this week.

SARAH: You could be the best dealer in the room if you wanted.

IAN: What's that got to do with what I'm saying to you?

SARAH: A lot. Charm won't get my knickers off.

IAN: What's behind that double glazing, Sarah?

SARAH: What d'you mean?

IAN: What you put up. When I go back to my flat I play back the answerphone in case someone's left a message. Hoping, more like. Never happens. You ever sat in a pub and pretended you're waiting for someone for the benefit of the others in there? I'm a long way from home, Sarah. I'm lonely. What do you do?

SARAH: There's always lots to do.

IAN: Like what? [*Pause.*] I said like what?

SARAH: Friends drop round. Drag me out to dinner. An Italian place in Camden. The veal's really good there. And the house red. We go through bottles of that. We've been friends a long time. There's four of us. We never stop laughing.

IAN: Bullshit. You always stay late in the dealing room. I watch you, remember.

SARAH: I like my work.

IAN: Is that all you've got? [*Pause.*] Sorry . . . didn't mean to come across so blunt.

SARAH: I'm quite happy being in the picture, taking corporate treasurers out to lunch. I'm just . . . sick of going to sleep at night with the radio on.

IAN: You as well, eh?

SARAH: I listen to the phone-ins. LBC.

IAN: That nutter from Purley who rings in every night.

SARAH: "Everything's been downhill since decimalization. Bring back pounds, shillings and pence."

IAN: He's got a point. [*Pause.*] I'm kidding. We could meet.

SARAH: Meet?

IAN: Go out.

SARAH: All right.

IAN: Where d'you fancy?

SARAH: A film'd be nice.

IAN: Anything you like.

SARAH: Would it be more than once — us going out?

IAN: I hope so. Don't you?

SARAH: We could share some chocolate in the dark.

IAN: Eh?

SARAH: At the cinema.

IAN: As long as it's not Revels. I only like the coconut ones. [*Pause.*] I'd cuddle you.

SARAH: Yes please.

[JIMMY *arrives.*]

JIMMY: [*singing a football chant*] You'll never take the Royal Enclosure, you'll never take the Royal Enclosure! Good this, innit?

IAN: We'll make an anarchist of you yet.

JIMMY: You must have dropped this in the box.

[*He hands* IAN *a chequebook.*]

SARAH: He didn't drop it, he discarded it. Anarchic gesture.

JIMMY: Your stubs make interesting reading.

IAN: They're private.

JIMMY: All those cheques to Mum and Dad. No wonder you've never got fuck all for yourself.

IAN: What's it got to do with you?

JIMMY: What is it up there — War on Want?

SARAH: Leave it, Jimmy. Go and pat a horse or something.

IAN: [*to* SARAH] The money just helps. Meat instead of tinned shit, new shoes for me sister. Necks just above the midden.

SARAH: So the better you do the better they do. Maybe you should stop being a fish out of water. Maybe you should stop wriggling. Give yourself up to it. Then we'd really be a pair.

[NICK *and* CUTTER *arrive.*]

NICK: Come on — out with the claret and the crab pâté!

JIMMY: Claret, eh? I've never drunk it but I've worn the scarf.

NICK: What?

CUTTER: He's a West Ham supporter.

NICK: My God, it's come to something when the mob are in need of Moss Bros. You look a bit subdued, Ian.

IAN: I couldn't find any corned beef.

NICK: My friend Julian took one look at you lot and thought you must have been Yob-a-Gram or something.

CUTTER: Your friend Julian was having each way bets. No balls, the upper class. He didn't even know what a forecast was.

JIMMY: Is that what you had?

CUTTER: A forecast, two doubles and a treble. Gambling isn't for the fainthearted.

NICK: I suppose you're going to tell us that's why you're the cable dealer.

CUTTER: You've just done it for me.

JIMMY: Did you crack it off?

CUTTER: I broke the bookie's heart.

JIMMY: If I touch you I might get lucky.
[*He does so.*]

SARAH: You need more than luck.

JIMMY: I know.
[CROSS *arrives.*]

CROSS: [*to* CUTTER] You'd better check you've still got your winnings — he probably tried to pocket them.

JIMMY: Save it for a rainy day, shouldn't he?

CUTTER: Advising caution?

SARAH: [*handing* CROSS *her camera*] Take a picture of the five of us, Charlie.

NICK: The five marketeers! Everyone make sure they've got a glass in their hand.
[JIMMY *touches* SARAH *up.*]

SARAH: Watch it!

NICK: I said glass, Jimmy.
[NICK *starts pouring the claret.*]

IAN: I'm not sure if I fancy being photographed in a compromising position with a hamper. A hampster, yes . . .

CROSS: Organise them, Graham.

CUTTER: Right, team photo. Jimmy, you kneeling down with me at the front, you three behind us with Sarah in the middle.
[*They arrange themselves.*]

CROSS: Ready when you are. Right — say greed!

ALL: Greed!
[*The photo is taken.*]

JIMMY: Right, let's get stuck into the fancies.
         [*They break up.* CUTTER *leads* SARAH *downstage
         while the others sit down ready to eat.*]

CUTTER: Thanks again for looking after me the other day, Sarah.
         It must have been quite scary.

SARAH: I was scared for you.

CUTTER: I'm grateful.
         [NICK *suddenly alerts the rest of them.*]

NICK: It's the Queen! She's arrived, she's coming this way!
         [*They start jockeying for position.*]

CROSS: Right, you're ambassadors for the Bank — don't forget
         that. If she stops to talk to anyone just say Ma'am at the
         end of every sentence.

NICK: I'll be the spokesman. She's only used to dealing with
         the high-born. Jimmy, you'd better stay in the back-
         ground.

JIMMY: Sod off — I won't get the chance to see her again till
         I'm knighted.

IAN: Don't even off-the-cuff conversations have to be
         arranged days beforehand? We'd have been informed.

CUTTER: What's the form anyway – when she walks past?

SARAH: You lot take your hats off and I curtsey.

NICK: Here she comes, here she comes.
         [*They remove their hats.* SARAH *curtseys.*]

JIMMY: I'm doffing my hat to the Queen. I've never doffed my
         hat before. I've never had a hat. Who says I'm vulgar?

CROSS: She's waving.

NICK: I've seen that dress before.

IAN: There'll always be an England.

NICK: You can scoff, but whatever else this country's become
         we've still got the Crown.

CUTTER: There's nothing like the sight of her face to bring out
         the patriotism in you.

SARAH: Patriotism? How many Sterling crises have you pre-
         sided over?

CROSS: He led the market then.

CUTTER: If the pound's weak you sell it. Sterling crisis is not my
         fault.

IAN: Half of it is.

NICK: Yes, don't be modest.

JIMMY: What would happen to Sterling if she died suddenly?

CROSS: Long-standing monarch, symbol of stability, unifying force of the Commonwealth — the market wouldn't give a fuck.

> [*A voice off shouts: "Three cheers for the Queen."
> The assembled group respond in unison: "Hip hip
> hooray!"*]

SCENE THREE

A railway platform. Train announcements. CROSS *and* SARAH.

SARAH: Who's going where, Charlie?

CROSS: I don't know what you're talking about.

SARAH: Now it's your turn to start owning up.

CROSS: But it's not your turn to be told anything.

SARAH: There'll have to be changes, won't there? Still, there's no shortage of talent.

CROSS: What's your interest?

SARAH: Justice. The best man for the job. And we both know who that is, don't we?

CROSS: You're full of surprises, aren't you? [*Pause.*] If there's any recommendations to make, I'll make them, all right?

> [*They exit.* NICK *appears. He crouches down behind
> a British Rail rubbish bin and starts to cut two lines
> of coke.* CUTTER *is being wheeled across the stage on
> a luggage trolley by* JIMMY. *They are all still in their
> Ascot garb.*]

JIMMY: I'm going to get changed.

CUTTER: Changed?

JIMMY: Well, I ain't walking through Bethnal Green looking like this.

> [*He exits.* CUTTER *looks at* NICK *and what he's
> doing.* NICK *becomes aware of* CUTTER's *scrutiny.*]

NICK: Not exactly the soul of discretion.

CUTTER: That's disgusting.

NICK: Why?

CUTTER: You shouldn't do drugs. It's . . . wrong. The Bank'd take a dim view.

NICK: Oh, I see. It's all right to undermine an economy but shove something up your nose and it's beyond the pale.

CUTTER: You'll get caught. Don't you care?

NICK: All I care about right now is a 125 rattling through and this blowing all over the place. I don't want my Charlie arriving at Euston before I do. Actually, this is a very reliable form of public transport — it gets me into work. I have to take the District Line followed by the Central Line. I have to. I'm not like Jimmy — I buy my confidence.

CUTTER: This is supposed to be a day off.

NICK: There's no such thing. And anyway, this gets moreish. You could do with something like it.

CUTTER: Being the cable dealer is addictive, anyway. I'm thirty now and I still feel like a kid who's learnt how to break into cars. I can joyride and take whatever's inside as long as I don't get caught.

NICK: Typical of you that your analogies are about delinquency.

CUTTER: It's what I came from.

NICK: I wake up scared I'm not going to spot a changing price or be caught long when everyone else is selling. I hate dealing. I loathe it.

CUTTER: Why stay, then?

NICK: It's a sort of . . . responsibility. [*Pause.*] In my family one keeps one's end up. When we gather for dinner we are professionally the armed forces, the medical profession and the City. My two elder brothers — one's a marine major, the other's a consultant obstetrician — have labradors and daughters in gymkhanas. The talk, when we're together, isn't about how much money we're earning — we're all far too anally retentive for that. What matters is the feeling, related in jokey anecdotes, that we occupy important territory in this country. My father, an ex-merchant banker, smokes his pipe and presides over the significance of all this. Mind you, he's never quite forgiven me for not joining Montague's. I'd like to stray even further away. The other two have no qualms about their ... inheritance. [*Pause.*] I make sauces, you know.

CUTTER: You make what?

NICK: I want to be a chef.

CUTTER: You in a kitchen?

NICK: We're supposed to live in a meritocracy, aren't we — where the humble can make a bundle? Why can't it work the other way round, why can't I make my father understand? [*Pause.*] If you wanted to come round one evening I could make a menu up – bread and butter pudding as a concession to your background. How's that sound?

CUTTER: I'll give it some thought.

NICK: It's easy to own up about my frailties to you because you've got your own, haven't you? Common ground the pair of us, eh?

CUTTER: What are you talking about?

NICK: The downfall of your duodenum. The afflicted, Graham — me and you.

CUTTER: It means nothing.

NICK: It must hurt you.

CUTTER: There's an unspoken law in the Bank — if dealing wasn't making you ill you wouldn't be doing your job properly.

NICK: Oh yes? And when you can't do your job properly because you're ill, you become a liability.

CUTTER: Not me.

NICK: Immune, are we?

CUTTER: It's intense, like being in a fire. I've got disfigured a bit but I don't care.

NICK: Don't you?
         [*Pause.*]

CUTTER: What else can I do? [*Pause.*] Who told you about me?
         [SARAH *appears with Maxpac coffees, sandwiches, etc.*]

NICK: Jimmy. But she set the ball rolling.

SARAH: It wasn't fair to everybody else.
CUTTER: Teamwork?
SARAH: We've all got a responsibility to the Bank.
CUTTER: Bollocks. All you were really worried about is how it might affect you. If my cable prices stop being competitive, the corporates stop ringing you and your reputation suffers, not to mention your commission. Your instinct was I might be at risk, I might be at risk because of him. And do you know where this insight comes from? I wouldn't suffer on anyone else's account either. I'd betray weakness if it threatened me.
NICK: You would?
CUTTER: What's it like, Sarah — to have me as a mirror held up to you?
SARAH: I'm better than you think.
CUTTER: You've put me on the receiving end. It's a funny feeling.
         [JIMMY *appears, having appropriated a train guard's hat and whistle. He blows it.*]
JIMMY: Stand back — train approaching!

SCENE FOUR

MILLAR *with a telephone and some paperwork.*

MILLAR: Obviously a simple high street bank like you isn't used to dealing with business transactions. You've converted my marks into Sterling but it's not the right amount. Yes, I know about your commission — but one hundred and forty-nine thousand Deutschmarks represents a hell of a lot more pounds than you've credited me with. Because I worked out the rate . . . two ninety-seven. What do you mean – not any more? Look, I'll have you know my daughter's a currency expert. I'll get her onto you — she'll soon put you right. [*Pause.*] What have the West German interest rates got to do with my umbrellas? The Bundesbank announced a cut in rates . . . who are the Bundesbank?

SCENE FIVE

The dealing room. JIMMY, NICK, SARAH, IAN *and* CROSS.

JIMMY: Every cloud has a silver lining.

IAN: Shut up.

NICK: I think he's actually going to enjoy it.

JIMMY: No good being squeamish about progress.

CROSS: OK — change stations.

[JIMMY *gets up and heads for the cable seat as* CUTTER *enters.*]

CUTTER: Morning.

CROSS: No, Jimmy.

JIMMY: What d'you mean, no?

CROSS: I didn't recommend you for the cable duties.

JIMMY: What?

CUTTER: What's going on?

CROSS: You've got it in you but not yet. You haven't got enough experience.

JIMMY: I'm not staying on Australian dollar — it's a fucking backwater.

CROSS: You're going to deal yen in future.

JIMMY: Who gets Cutter's job, then? Nick's out — are you bringing in someone?

CUTTER: What the fuck's going on?

NICK: Musical chairs. A sordid version. I'm sorry.

SARAH: [*to* IAN] Go on.

[IAN *gets up and heads towards the cable seat.*]

JIMMY: Ian!

CUTTER: I'm here now.

NICK: His hair shirt's come off.

JIMMY: [*to* IAN] Someone's put you up to this.

SARAH: He put himself up. He wants to be in the picture.

CUTTER: I sit there.

NICK: [*to* SARAH] You two are cosy all of a sudden.

JIMMY: He must be knocking her off.

IAN: Shut it!

NICK: Ian — you really are a horse that gets darker by the minute.

IAN: There's some people I love and I'm not going to let them live hand to mouth . . .

JIMMY: Don't kid yourself. You're doing it for you.

IAN: I'm already part of things here anyway so you could say it's in for a penny in for a pound.

CUTTER: I'm the fucking cable dealer!

CROSS: Sit down, Ian — it's where you belong now.

CUTTER: I . . . belong.

IAN: Lord George Brown, travelling first class on a plane, the worse for wear on champagne, asked by a journalist about his socialist ideals and where they'd gone, replied defensively in a slurred voice, "Listen, I'll have you know I was born in one room." [*Pause.*] I've learnt a trick or two in this one.

CUTTER: Promotion, Charlie. Tell me that's what's happening to me.

CROSS: Don't be naive.

CUTTER: It's not naivety.

CROSS: What then — optimism? Have you seen your P and L figures for the last month?

CUTTER: They'll pick up.

CROSS: You've seen me watching you. I even tried to warn you. I wish you'd tried to protect yourself but instead you just shrugged off every danger signal. You were so fucking short-sighted, so . . . complacent.

SARAH: You should have seen this coming.

CUTTER: [*to* CROSS] You've sold me.

CROSS: I tried to defend you! But South saw I'd been carrying dead weight for too long. Now it's cast a doubt on my judgement. Ironic, isn't it? I've offered my resignation this morning.

CUTTER: You put yourself on the line for me?
                    [*Pause.*]

SARAH: Tell him the rest, Charlie.

CROSS: I went to lunch at Nomura. They've offered me a job. I think my future's with the Japanese now. [*Pause.*] I got sentimental about you, fair-minded they used to say. Got me into trouble — so I made sure I got myself out.

CUTTER: Always political.

CROSS: Looking everywhere. I told you I liked my survival.

CUTTER: You've fallen on your feet, then. I've just . . . fallen.

CROSS: You're slower now but it's not just your age that's killed you as a dealer, it's your arrogance. You even stopped knowing when to cut out at a loss because your ego wouldn't allow you to.

JIMMY: [*picking up the phone*] Barclays Hong Kong cable!

IAN: Fifty-five/sixty!

CUTTER: I call cable!

JIMMY: [*down the phone*] Fifty-five/sixty! [*to* IAN] Yours!

CUTTER: I've sat through wars, assassinations and a financial crash at that desk — I've never been touched once. I picked up at least half a cent on everything that happened, turning it into thousands for this Bank. Why should I see anything coming? I had a very short past when I came here, I was only eighteen. I looked forward to the future and it all came true. It never stopped coming true. Why should I see anything coming? My wife became an eyesore and my guts fill up with acid. Drawbacks. Occupational hazards. The only ones. Why should I see anything coming? All I believe in is the market — the rest of the world's out of focus. Why should I see anything coming? When things started going wrong I refused to look. I'm scared . . . why should I see anything coming?

JIMMY: This game we're in, it's a bit like pass the parcel, innit? You take and sell on at a profit. Now every time the music stops you're caught holding. I used to love watching you.

CUTTER: There's a hundred banks that'd have me as its cable dealer — no problem!

JIMMY: They wouldn't let you deal the Polish zloty. Reputations get around this market as fast as the rumours about the pimples on Reagan's nose.

CUTTER: I never considered you lot a threat.

JIMMY: Never saw it coming?

CUTTER: I never thought you'd dare. I thought you were all bigger messes than me. And something else, something almost funny . . . I thought you liked me. Nick — you understand frailty. Help me.

NICK: I'm taking over from Charlie. From performance to responsibility.

CUTTER: Responsibility — you?

NICK: Don't spoil it for me, it's going to help me. I've always liked to give the impression that my progress has been graceful, effortless. You know better. Now I'll be out of the fire, supervising it. Anxious not to queer the pitch and all that.

CUTTER: Sarah? You said to me, "I'm better than you think." Are you?

SARAH: My light's on — I've got to answer the phone. [*Pause.*] Dollar/mark virgin.

NICK: Seventy/eighty!

SARAH: [*down the phone*] Seventy/eighty! [*to* NICK] Ten bucks at eighty!

CUTTER: Speak up for me.

SARAH: I can't let up for a minute.

CUTTER: I'm quite frightened.

SARAH: I can't let up for a minute.

CUTTER: You too, Ian?

IAN: If I'd have said no, they'd have poached someone from another bank.

CUTTER: Better the devil you know, eh?

IAN: I thought I was immune.

CUTTER: Get up.

IAN: It's too late.

CUTTER: That's my seat. Get up, you cunt!
                [*He grabs* IAN *and tries to pull him off.*]
        You can't take it away from me! You can't!
                [JIMMY *and* CROSS *pull* CUTTER *off and restrain him by the arms. The struggle is quite vicious. Eventually they subdue him.*]

JIMMY: He's cracked up! I knew he couldn't hack it.

NICK: It's grief, you prat!

SARAH: Let him go.

JIMMY: He'll whack Ian if we do.

IAN: I don't mind. Why shouldn't he?

CUTTER: I'm not going to hit anyone.

JIMMY: Nick, your light's on.

NICK: [*on the phone, addressing* JIMMY] It's Midland London, they want a price on dollar/yen.

JIMMY: [*to* CUTTER] No more trouble-making?

CUTTER: Shut up, you little cunt.

> [JIMMY *and* CROSS *let go of* CUTTER. JIMMY *goes to his screen.*]

JIMMY: [*to* NICK] Forty-three/fifty!

NICK: [*down the phone*] Forty-three/fifty! [*to* JIMMY] Lose five.

> [JULIE *enters.*]

JULIE: Hello Graham — sorry to hear about your news. [*to* CROSS] Where d'you want to put me?

CROSS: Ask Nick — he's going to be your new boss.

> [NICK *indicates* JIMMY's *former station.*]

JIMMY: [*to* CUTTER] Julie's becoming a trainee dealer on probation. Australian.

JULIE: Stepping into Jimmy's shoes. I'm thrilled. I never thought I'd be anything other than a Telex girl.

JIMMY: Everyone gets a chance here.

JULIE: [*to* CUTTER] You've been doing this a long time, haven't you? I was wondering if there was any advice you could give me before you go?

SCENE SIX

The dealing room. JULIE, SARAH, NICK, IAN *and* JIMMY.

JULIE: Sarah . . . reception have got someone downstairs for you. A Mr. Millar.

JIMMY: A relative?

SARAH: Just a namesake. Just a . . . client.

JULIE: Well — what shall I tell them?

SARAH: He'll have to wait. Or make an appointment for some other time.

JULIE: [*down the phone*] Miss Millar's unavailable at the moment. [*Pause.*] He'll wait.

IAN: Ten yours!

JIMMY: You're coping well. I wonder how long it'll last.

IAN: Long enough.

JIMMY: You're just going short on Sterling at the moment. Joining the bandwagon on a falling pound.

NICK: Had to happen sometime. Devaluation of the dollar's over — they've depressed domestic demand, now they want their fellow Americans to go out and start buying dishwashers again.

SARAH: Make them feel they're in less of a recession.

NICK: Mind you, they'll be hard to convince. It's part of American folklore — after a crash there's always a slump.

JIMMY: [*reading from the screen*] British industry costs up five per cent on last month!

NICK: You know why that is, don't you? No bloody wage restraint.

SARAH: It'll hurt exports even more.

IAN: The pound needs to go lower — selling it is a one-way bet.

JULIE: But Sterling was so strong last year.

IAN: The dollar was so weak, you mean and the Bundesbank were buying the buck against the Deutschmark as intervention.

NICK: He means our fortunes were camouflaged.

JIMMY: Ours?

NICK: Sorry — I mean the United Kindom's.

IAN: Now our trade deficit's really beginning to sink in. Two things — an overvalued exchange rate — yet again — and the fact that we've stopped being able to make anything.

NICK: Here endeth today's lesson.

IAN: I'm right, though, aren't I? All the forecasts were over-optimistic.

SARAH: Nigel did say there might be a huge margin of error. In other words we might catch something nasty from America.

IAN: We have.

JIMMY: Look — fuck all this analysis — Ian's just having a good day because someone's fucked it somewhere else.

IAN: You don't think I can handle this at all, do you? It's a long time since I got off the Inter-City train, Jimmy. We don't all come to London and end up sleeping on Euston station. I'm in the picture now. I'm the fucking cable dealer.

JULIE: Cable, Bank of Chicago!

IAN: Forty/forty-five!

JULIE: [*down the phone*] Forty/forty-five! [*to* IAN] Twenty-five yours!

IAN: [*to* NICK] Way it's going, Sterling's set to end up three cents down by the end of the day's trading.

NICK: The market's pointing its accusing finger here now.

IAN: How much lower d'you think it'll go?

NICK: Bank of England hasn't given any signals.

IAN: Let's see how far it'll fall before something happens.

NICK: You mean how far we can take it?

IAN: Sell it down the river.

JULIE: Won't that make things even worse?

IAN: So what? Serve the government right.

NICK: Trust you to try and make it sound like an act of subversion. You just want to lead the market, don't you?

IAN: Yes.

JIMMY: You might start a run on the pound but you won't make any money on it once the market's alerted because no one'll want to buy them off you.

IAN: The market doesn't have to be alerted.

NICK: Forget it.

JULIE: Wouldn't the Bank of England want to intervene after a bit?

NICK: That's right. They might want to see it lower but they wouldn't want it to get out of hand. If they come in and support it in the middle of a selling operation we're stuck with a whole load of dollars we'd have to get rid of at a loss.

IAN: Look, apart from what the authorities want, the market's losing confidence in Sterling because it's losing confidence in the economy, right? When that sentiment

SARAH: starts racing they can come in and buy all the pounds they like — they've got no chance.

SARAH: But there's also seven countries' finance ministers who keep saying they want to see stable exchange rates.

IAN: Concerted intervention didn't help the dollar much last year, did it?

SARAH: But this is different.

IAN: How?

SARAH: This time they ... they mean it. [*Pause.*] After the Crash they won't have the markets behaving like rogue elephants again. There's an agreement ... the market knows that and it might make the market cautious. It might not follow you.

IAN: A sure thing's hard to resist. And anyway, those ministers can't even agree on who stands where for the official photographs. Co-ordinate their economic policies? The market still holds them all to ransom.

JIMMY: What's got into him — you?

SARAH: I don't have to. That seat's generating enough heat.

NICK: You want to go up to your limit?

IAN: I was thinking more of the section's limit.

NICK: You must be joking.

IAN: We can sell the pound at one seventy-two, then buy it back at one sixty-eight, sixty-seven fifty, even. Then it'll go on dropping like a man who's lost his parachute. The market's nervous; it'd only need the smallest signal and there'd be a stampede.

NICK: What signal?

IAN: We'll put a rumour into the brokers.

JIMMY: North Sea Oil's dried up.

JULIE: Has it?

IAN: No, but it peaked in '85-'86.

SARAH: But no one's started panicking about it yet. Why don't you make them face up to it — say a rig's been blown up, a major field has caught fire?

IAN: Not bad, not bad. But you see what I mean, Nick, we can make all this gloom work for us.

JULIE: Make a bad thing worse.

IAN: [*a sudden idea*] Thatcher at the eye hospital, remember?

JIMMY: Dodgy minces.

IAN: That's right. Apart from the fucking myopia.

NICK: I'm not with you, I'm afraid.

IAN: Standing down for health reasons!

SARAH: No fourth-term Thatch.

IAN: Handing over to Parkinson or Baker or someone. The market'll shit itself.

NICK: If it believed it.

IAN: The mood the market's in, it'd believe anything that's bad for Britain.

SARAH: He's right, Nick.

JIMMY: I've underestimated him.

IAN: Nick, it's no good just pontificating. We won't just be taking a few points, we'd be making cents. The profit'll be enormous.

NICK: There wasn't supposed to be as much pressure on me. Just planning and watching.

IAN: The pressure'll be on me. You just have to make the decision.

NICK: I've only ever decided what I was going to do before.

IAN: Fucking hell Nick, you've got a new job now!

NICK: We'll be risking a lot of money.

SARAH: Don't we always?

IAN: And anyway, what sort of coach tells his players to take it easy?

NICK: All right. Sell four hundred million.

JIMMY: Nice one.

NICK: Fucking hell.

IAN: Nick, you'll have to help deal.

NICK: We'll need to use Sarah as well.

IAN: [*to* SARAH] Will you?

SARAH: I can't wait.

[*She takes up the vacant dealing chair.*]

IAN: [*addressing the others*] Right — we're going to deal via the screens. It's just bank to bank — that way the market can't catch on. There's five of us so we'll do twenty quid deals four times each. Jimmy — you hit the Japanese banks, Sarah the French, Julie the Australian.

I'll do Citibank, Chemical and Co. and Nick — can you
hit Frankfurt? You know the drill — "Hi hi friends, how
is the cable dollar spot?" Whatever their bid price for
Sterling is, give it. Start punting.

SARAH: Juicy fucker.

> [*We see them set to work on their keyboards,
> punching out enquiries onto their screens that they
> are watching intently. Within seconds they get re-
> sponses.*]

First deal done.

JIMMY: And again.

JULIE: Me as well.

NICK: Dollars to me.

SARAH: Banque de Lyons at one seventy-two twenty!

JIMMY: Nomura quoting twenty-five/thirty-five! I'm having five
quids' worth!

IAN: Thank you and bye-bye for now, First National Bank of
Chicago!

NICK: What's the pound doing in the market?

JULIE: I've just had a bid price of twenty-five from Westpac.

IAN: Sterling's steady in the brokers.

JIMMY: What do we do when we're through?

IAN: When you've got rid of eighty quid, hold on.

NICK: You better get this right.

IAN: We can't lose.

SARAH: I've hit my four.

JIMMY: Japanese takeaway my last twenty quid. Be my sushi,
baby.

NICK: Holding all dollars now. Eighty long.

IAN: Julie?

JULIE: The price is just coming through from Westpac. I've hit
the left-hand side, now I'm telling them thank you and
bye-bye for now.

SARAH: So we're holding, what . . . about 680 million dollars
now.

JULIE: The brokers are quoting fifteen/twenty now . . . it's
starting to slip again.

IAN: Right, brokers everybody! Phones! I'll do Godsall, Nick
— you call Marshalls; Jimmy — your usual. Sarah, they

won't know you so don't bother. Julie — any of the rest.
Sound convincing for fuck's sake!

    [*They pick up the phones and we hear them giving
    the news about the Prime Minister.*]

NICK: Monkey . . . can you confirm something for me . . . ?
We've got a dealer here whose brother is a registrar at
Moorfields Eye Hospital. Says the Prime Minister's
been secretly admitted for another eye operation.

JIMMY: What's this about the Thatch going blind, Martin . . . ?
Who's her deputy?

JULIE: Isn't it sad about the Prime Minister — just when she
was getting things moving . . .

IAN: Thatcher's private office has just rung the Press
Association . . . there's going to be a statement about
her health . . .

NICK: Of course it hasn't come through on Reuters yet. It's
supposed to be a secret.

JIMMY: We're going to stop trading here till there's clarification
— Sterling'll have no chance. I fancy Heseltine me-
self . . . I like self-made millionaires.

JULIE: Her resignation's expected this afternoon. What will the
country do now, eh?

IAN: All public engagements have been cancelled.

    [*They put the phones down.*]

Light the blue touch paper and retire.

SARAH: We're all going to end up in the Tower.

    [*Pause.*]

JIMMY: Barclays and Deutsche Bank have just changed their
price.

IAN: The panic's started already.

JIMMY: We're getting one seventy-two Sterling bid now, Ian.

NICK: That's fifteen points it's dropped already.

IAN: I told you.

JIMMY: I'm hearing seventy/eighty out of the brokers now!

SARAH: Forty/fifty from the Banque de Lyons!

NICK: Jesus Christ.

IAN: The market's running scared. It's getting rid of its
Sterling.

JULIE: One seventy-one Sterling bid!

JIMMY: Seventy/eighty!

NICK: It won't go much lower.

IAN: Yes it will.

JIMMY: Sixty-one to six!

SARAH: That's one and a half cents it's lost in less than a minute.

JULIE: Does the market always act like this?

IAN: Yes, yes, yes!

JIMMY: New price for Chemical — forty-three/fifty!

NICK: Sell your dollars now — before it starts to go the other way.

IAN: Not yet. We'll make more money if we wait.

NICK: You're being greedy.

IAN: I'm speculating. I'm not going to blow this opportunity.

JIMMY: Touching a dollar sixty-nine, now. The pound's going to fall out of bed!

IAN: You see, Nick. No one wants to hold Sterling.

JULIE: Down another twenty points!

SARAH: Be careful, Ian.

JIMMY: Ninety/figure! It's lost four cents in three minutes! I wonder what the Bank of England are doing.

NICK: Don't you dare get caught by any sudden announcements.

IAN: All right, cable calls now, please! Let's turn it round, let's pass the parcel!

[*They get on the phones.*]

NICK: Cable please.

JIMMY: Can I have a spot for cable?

JULIE: Quote for cable!

SARAH: What are you calling cable?

NICK: [*to* IAN] Eighty/eighty-seven!

IAN: Mine!

NICK: [*down the phone*] Twenty-five mine!

JIMMY: Seventy-five/eighty!

IAN: Take five!

JIMMY: [*down the phone*] Twenty-five mine.

SARAH: It's still going down! Lloyds have stopped quoting!

JULIE: Sixty-two/sixty-nine!

IAN: Mine!

JULIE: [*down the phone*] I pay for Sterling in twenty-five.

IAN: Buy it all back now at whatever prices you hear! Keep buying till you're flat!

[*The subsequent calls are made down the phone.*]

IAN: Mine!

NICK: Mine!

JIMMY: Mine!

SARAH: Mine!

JULIE: Mine!

IAN: Mine!

NICK: Mine!

JIMMY: Mine!

SARAH: Mine!

JULIE: Mine!

IAN: Mine!

NICK: Mine!

JIMMY: Mine!

JULIE: Mine!

[IAN *has the final word.*]

IAN: Mine and I'm out!

[*Cheers and jubilation.*]

JIMMY: The pound's new level — one sixty-six forty and falling.

SARAH: [*kissing* IAN] Congratulations!

JIMMY: [*shaking* IAN's *hand*] You might have a future after all.

JULIE: Sarah . . . reception want to know if you're ready to see that bloke yet.

SARAH: Tell them I'm not here. Tell them I've gone home. I can't see him!

JULIE: [*down the phone*] She's gone home. [*Pause; to* IAN] How much money d'you think you made?

NICK: He made a killing.

IAN: About eight million pounds if my maths are right.

JIMMY: Three per cent dealer's commission on that can't be bad, eh?

IAN: I led the market. I feel . . . important. [*to* JIMMY] You'll fucking take me seriously now, eh?

NICK: Carpetbagger.

[NICK *is looking in his pocket, fumbling for something.*]

JIMMY: You stopped sniping, then?

IAN: What's the point?

SARAH: Let's celebrate.

IAN: What — my new realism?

NICK: I've got to get out . . . go out.

> [*He hurries towards the exit, holding an envelope. As he does so,* MILLAR *appears. In his eagerness to get out,* NICK *brushes past* MILLAR *and consequently drops the envelope. Cocaine is scattered on the floor.*]

MILLAR: [*to* SARAH] I knew you were here.

JIMMY: Shall I ring security?

SARAH: I meant to call you.

MILLAR: Slip your mind, did it? I can't get it out of mine.

SARAH: It was bad advice. Unprofessional.

MILLAR: This is your father you're talking to! [*Pause.*] I've had to lay four of my people off. I had to do that to them — I'd budgeted for a profit margin that didn't happen. Nothing extravagant — just the difference between what we made them for and what I thought I was selling them at. Sounds so simple, doesn't it?

SARAH: I'm sorry the Deutschmark went the other way.

MILLAR: And that's all.

SARAH: It's just that I'm used to taking risks here. It's my job.

MILLAR: Currency fluctuation wasn't the only thing I didn't get protection from. I needed protection against you.

JIMMY: Your light's on, Sarah.

SARAH: We can't talk here. It's always so busy. I'm busy now.

MILLAR: I see. [*Pause.*] I feel like I've lost you to some bad religion.

> [*He makes to go.*]

SARAH: Dad, please . . .

JULIE: Look what's just come up on the screens.

JIMMY: The market's overshot again! Bank of England threatening to raise interest rates to take pressure off the pound.

> [MILLAR *has gone.*]

SARAH: [*a cry*] Dad, please!

> [NICK *is on his knees gathering up the powder and trying to put it back in the envelope. He looks up and*

finds JIMMY *standing over him, watching.* SARAH *is in tears.* IAN *reaches out a hand to console her.* JULIE *looks on.*]

JULIE: The pound's going up slightly. Isn't this a good time to start buying Sterling again?

SCENE SEVEN

A street. Various pieces of household furniture are assembled on the side of the street. JIMMY *is standing by it, anxiously watching something across the way.* SARAH *appears.*

SARAH: What are you doing here?

JIMMY: I drove him up. He said it was an emergency. A friend in need and all that.

SARAH: You — a friend?

JIMMY: We like each other. More now. Now we see eye to eye.

SARAH: What on earth can he have in common with you?

JIMMY: You're his girlfriend — what's so odd about me being his mate? [*Pause.*] D'you think my car'll be all right over there?

SARAH: They're just curious.

JIMMY: The way they're looking at it anyone'd think it was a fucking spacecraft. It's like the seventies up here, innit?

SARAH: The kids are just the same as where you come from. So is everyone.
     [*Pause.*]

JIMMY: You got his message, then?

SARAH: Only that he'd gone home. What's been going on?

JIMMY: Well, it ain't spring cleaning.

SARAH: Where are his parents?

JIMMY: He's gone looking for them.
     [IAN *appears.*]

  IAN: Why did you come?

SARAH: You sounded so upset on the phone.

  IAN: I knew this would happen.

SARAH: What do you mean, you knew? Where are they?

  IAN: I don't know.

SARAH: I thought you were helping.

IAN: I got a call from my kid sister. Crying. Some men had come.

SARAH: What men?

IAN: D'you remember when the interest rates went up?

JIMMY: You mean they had a mortgage on this?

IAN: Buy your own council house they were told. They were all for it.

JIMMY: Interests rates go down sometimes . . . you win some, you lose some.

IAN: They didn't realise they were sitting on a roulette wheel. They wanted to know why this sort of thing always seems to be happening.

SARAH: Interest rates went up two per cent after you led the market.

IAN: I talked like it was an achievement. They . . . couldn't see it.

JIMMY: What's this worth — only about thirty grand, innit?

IAN: About.

JIMMY: The extra repayment's nothing on that, is it?

IAN: That's what I said. Especially with my bigger cheques going into their account.

SARAH: I thought that was a sensitive point.

IAN: Got even more sensitive once I'd said it. [*Pause.*] This house has never seen so much rowing. If I was forgetting myself they were being ungrateful. My dad wanted to throw me out of the door, my mother said it was undignified. She always had a great sense of dignity. Anyway, after that the bank started sending back the cheques I was paying into the account. My mum and dad had changed their number, changed their bank. I tried to talk to them but they wouldn't listen.

JIMMY: This stereo ain't bad.

IAN: A Christmas present I bought. When they left they must have taken everything they needed. Wanted. They obviously didn't want this.

JIMMY: I'll have it. Give us a price.
          [*Pause.*]

IAN: Forty quid . . . thirty-five . . .

JIMMY: Mine!

SARAH: Ian!

IAN: I've made my bed . . . Anyway, my money's not good enough for them any more. Refused on principle. [*Pause.*] How can you have principles against your own son?

SARAH: The arrears must have built up. Why haven't you let on there was anything wrong?

IAN: I was hoping to make it up with them.

JIMMY: Shame they couldn't just learn to live with the market. I hope they're indoors somewhere — this rain.

[SARAH *puts an umbrella up.*]

IAN: Let's get under that.

SARAH: Bankrupt stock. Going cheap.

JIMMY: I'll have some. Give us a price.

IAN: Would he see you?

SARAH: No.

IAN: We're the pair you said we would be. Now we're not lonely.

SARAH: What have we done?

JIMMY: What have you done? [*Pause; as he walks off*] When you find your mum and dad, Ian, offer to bring them to London. That might do the trick. It's a fucking quicksand round here.

IAN: I don't like it outdoors any more.

[*They stand beneath the umbrella together. We hear the sound of the market again.*]

THE END